tommy walsh
DIY SURVIVAL

tommy walsh
DIYSURVIVAL

I dedicate this book to the memory of my Dad.
A better man has yet to walk the face of the Earth.

First published in 2002
This paperback edition published in 2003 by Collins
an imprint of HarperCollins*Publishers*
77–85 Fulham Palace Road, London, W6 8JB

everything clicks at:
www.collins.co.uk

Tommy Walsh photographs: Laurence Cendrowicz
All other photographs: Tim Ridley
Artworks: David Day and Robin Harris
Consultants and content planning: Step Editions
Design and editorial: Focus Publishing
Editor: Guy Croton
Designer: David Etherington

For HarperCollins
Managing Editor: Angela Newton
Art Direction: Luke Griffin

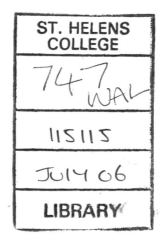

A CIP catalogue record for this book is available from the British Library

ISBN 0007164084

Colour reproduction by Butler & Tanner
Printed and bound in Great Britain

Please note: Always take care when embarking on any DIY project. Read the
instructions for tools before you commence, and take appropriate safety
precautions. Great care has been taken to ensure that the information contained
in this book is accurate and correct. However, the publishers and author can
accept no responsibility or liability for any loss or damage.

FOREWORD

A question I get asked regularly is 'What did you do before and how did you get on the telly?' I was, and still am, a hard landscaper/builder. I was recommended to a television producer, Carol Haslam, to carry out some re-modelling and restoration work on her period house in Hampstead. While I was working there, Carol asked me to review a couple of pilot programme tapes, one of which was the precursor to Ground Force called 'Over the Garden Wall'. The format was dire, and I told her so! The format and name were changed and Carol surprised me by asking if I would like to join the team. At first I refused, and when I told my wife Marie, and kids, Charlotte, Natalie and Jonjo, they all said, 'Dad, you must go on the telly!' I said 'No'. The following evening Charlotte confronted me and said, 'Dad, you have to go on television because I've had a bet with a boy at school who doesn't believe me!' I asked how much the bet was for (bear in mind she was only eight years old at the time). She said '£10.' In shock, I spat out the tea I was drinking and asked, 'How on earth are you going to pay that?' She stood up, folded her arms and said indignantly, 'Daddy, I don't intend to lose!' I couldn't stop laughing. I re-told the story to Carol – we both laughed and I said, 'OK'.

I did a screen test with somebody called Charlie Dimmock, who turned up looking like a librarian, hair up in a bun and wearing a long white cardi'.

Before you ask, I do not know whether she was in 'liberated mode' then or not! The BBC said 'Sign them up'. We only met Alan for the very first time on the morning we started filming. The rest, as they say, is history! I have always been a believer in fate, and I received a very large slice of good fortune on that occasion!

Everything I am I owe to my Mum and Dad. My Mum taught me to read at a very young age, and taught me discipline and respect. Dad was my mentor, taking me with him to work from the age of four. Dad taught me most of what I know, and particularly, not to take life too seriously. Treat others as you would want to be treated, laugh and have fun. He was my best friend, and I miss him more than I can say, but I know he was so, so proud of my success. I am sure he is still watching over me and guiding me somehow.

People often say to me, 'this must be better than being a builder'. Well it's hard work, but good fun. I love building and I will always be a builder first and anything else second, which probably confirms my old headmaster's prediction – 'Tommy Walsh, you'll end your days breaking stones!' (Although I think he may have meant something different!)

CONTENTS

INTRODUCTION

My wife Marie deserves the credit for the idea of this book. She planted the seed (excuse the pun!) so to speak, stating that because I'm working away so much, there's nobody to do the DIY repairs at home. She declared that she was going to purchase a DIY book and carry out the repairs herself. I have to admit, this idea produced a rather smug smile on my face, as the last time she carried out any DIY was over 27 years ago at her mother's house when she painted her bedroom blue. She really did paint everything in blue emulsion – including the walls, ceiling, wardrobes, skirtings, doors and window frames. She even coated the power points and light switches! This natural ability for DIY must run in the family, because her mum, Annie, my mother-in-law, once painted her bedroom carpet! My wife found all the books available too comprehensive, big and heavy. She even dropped one, it was so cumbersome.

My wife said to me, 'what's needed is a back to basics DIY book, something simple with everyday common tasks explained'. That set me thinking. I looked around and discovered there wasn't anything available along the lines I had in mind. My friends and people I work with know I can't be serious for very long, and living is much nicer with a smile on your face, so I wanted to incorporate some humour into the book to lift it, make it more enjoyable to read. I wanted the book to be informal, and different to other DIY books. What I find really irritating are books written by so-called experts, who address the reader in such a patronising manner that it makes them frightened to attempt the task. I have been in the building trade since I was a small boy with my father, and everyone makes mistakes – that's how we learn. My idea is to try and de-mystify DIY. I've tried to do this by writing anecdotes at the top of each task, of which there are 60. (Originally there were 42, but the publishers increased that to 60 – without any increase in the fee, I might add!) The anecdotes are a mixture of advice, inspiration

and autobiographical stories and cock-ups to try and demonstrate that it's not the end of the world if you make a mistake, and that DIY is not the exclusive domain of male professionals. I hope that everybody, even youngsters with supervision, feel (if they have the inclination) able to attempt some, if not all, the tasks within this book.

We, as a nation, have undergone huge social change since the 1960s. It was as if somebody altered the rules of the game. Couples don't endure bad marriages; lots of people don't even feel the need to get married any more – career-minded people who don't have time, or don't feel inclined to have a partner. It's well known, because of many different factors, that we are living longer. A lot of people in the past have either relied on their partner, or paid somebody to do the repairs for them. Finding a competent builder who's not busy, (remember any GOOD builder is always busy), and is interested in unblocking your sink, or changing a lamp holder, probably equates to winning the lottery in consecutive weeks! If you do happen to be lucky enough to find one of this rare breed, to accommodate your time and needs, you'll probably have to take out a second mortgage. What I aim to achieve with this book is: if it saves you the cost of one average call-out fee of £50, then you'll feel so pleased with yourself, you'll go out and buy four books with the savings to give to your friends as gifts, and then I might not have to take orders from Mr. T any more!

Seriously though, any DIY is a matter of planning the task properly before you start, and carrying it out comfortably in your own time. Build up your home tool kit over a period of time. Try to buy the best-quality tools that you can afford, and start off with small tasks to build your confidence. With the tools and materials available on the market today, you really will be surprised and amazed at what you can achieve. There is one thing I can guarantee, that there's not any feeling quite like it when you take on a task you've never done before and make a good job of it. Just stand back and admire it – you won't half feel proud.

DANGER! TOMMY AT WORK

BASIC TOOLS

Walk around any **DIY** store and you'll be amazed at the range of tools available. You could easily spend a fortune on fancy gadgets – and then spend hours trying to find homes for them all! In fact, you don't need that many tools to cope with most DIY projects, and you certainly won't need that many to tackle the projects in this book. A few general tools should get you through most tasks, and you can always hire specialist equipment like steam strippers or drain rods if you need them.

Over the next four pages I've tried to summarize most of the tools and fixings you are likely to encounter. Some of them are very general and multi-purpose – such as screwdrivers or spirit levels – while others may relate to specific jobs. Though you can get by without some things, never skimp when it comes to safety. Sturdy step ladders are a must for any job above eye level, and protective gloves, goggles and dust masks are vital for many tasks. Make sure your first aid kit is up-to-scratch, too – though hopefully you'll never need it. And my final tip – you don't need to spend a fortune on tools, but do buy the best you can afford. A quality screwdriver, saw or paintbrush will pay for itself in the long run, and will help you to produce better results.

GENERAL TOOLS

Some tools are useful for lots of things, and that's what most of these are. A sturdy tool box is a wise investment: not only does it mean you'll be able to find that hammer when you need it, it's also safely out of harm's way and isn't likely to jump out of a crowded cupboard at an inopportune moment.

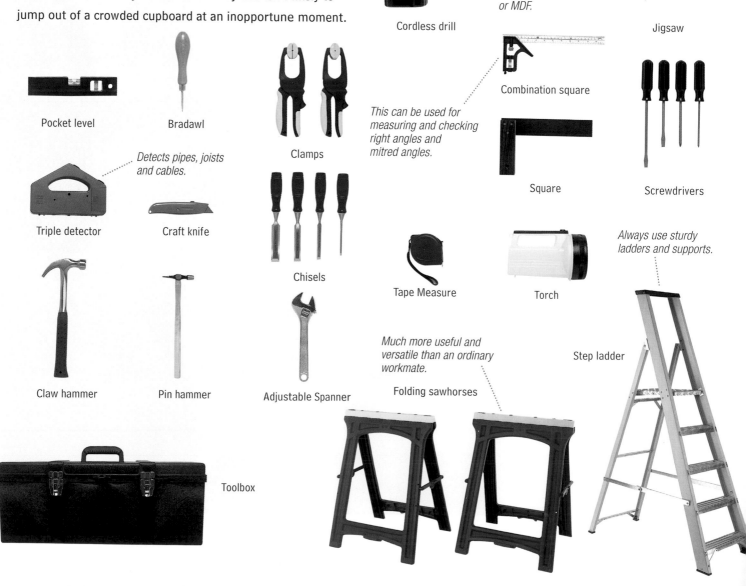

A cordless drill is very easy to use and will make light work of most jobs. Invaluable!

This is ideal for making curved cuts in timber or MDF.

Cordless drill

Jigsaw

Pocket level

Bradawl

This can be used for measuring and checking right angles and mitred angles.

Combination square

Clamps

Detects pipes, joists and cables.

Triple detector

Craft knife

Square

Screwdrivers

Chisels

Tape Measure

Torch

Always use sturdy ladders and supports.

Claw hammer

Pin hammer

Adjustable Spanner

Much more useful and versatile than an ordinary workmate.

Folding sawhorses

Step ladder

Toolbox

Panel saw

Mini hacksaw

Safety gear is vital for any job which puts your bodily safety at risk.

Protective gloves

Ear defenders

Tenon saw

Mitre saw

Dust mask

Safety glasses

PLUMBING TOOLS

Handy for cleaning blocked waste pipes.

Many of the tools here you should only need if, heaven forbid, you get a blockage somewhere. However, the wrenches are handy for holding pipe work or undoing nuts on taps. The radiator key is an invaluable little tool for curing those knocks and bangs in your heating system, so always keep one of these close to hand.

Hydraulic pump

Always handy!

This is specially designed for cleaning toilets and gully traps.

This is used to 'bleed' or release trapped air in a radiator.

Latex gloves

Radiator key

Auger

This is good for gripping onto pipework or damaged nuts – the adjusting screw at the end of the handle tightens the grip.

You can hire these for cleaning blocked drains.

Stillson wrench

Plier wrench

Basin wrench

Drain rods

Sealant gun

PAINT CHART

Painting can be fun or it can be a chore. Some people will happily lose a few hours with the radio on and a paintbrush in their hand, while others dread losing another weekend to the second coat. Part of the reason for this may be the end result. People who spend time getting the preparation right reap the benefits at the end and will enjoy taking their time with the job. People who want an instant effect, however, often end up with shoddy results, which disillusions them against ever taking on a decorating job again.

So the secret with painting, as with all decorating, is to take your time. Spend a while looking at paint charts and picking out colours. Take the time to clean, sand and prepare your surface properly (I look at this in greater detail on page 74), and make sure your work area is organized. Not properly covering or moving the furniture might seem like a shortcut at the beginning of the job, but it will certainly add time and stress to the day when you're desperately trying to sponge off vivid blue paint from your brand new sofa....

CHOOSING COLOURS

It's never easy quite getting the right shade. With so many ready-made and made-to-order colours available, the decision can be a daunting one. Luckily, paint manufacturers have realized this, and now sell small tester pots which are perfect for trying out at home, before making the decision to buy the full quantity. It's worth remembering that colours can have different effects on a room – warm colours will make the room feel cosy but smaller; pale colours can increase the feeling of spaciousness but may not be as comforting on a cold winter night. Of course,

clever use of lighting can also affect this, so do think about the room in its entirety, complete with furniture, natural light and artificial light, when choosing your paint.

Different types of paint have varying surface coverage qualities, whether they be oil- or water-based. To calculate how much you need, measure the area you wish to paint and work out the square meterage (length x width). When selecting your paints, check the coverage rate on the can to quantify how much you need. Always allow at least 10% extra paint because you do not want to run short.

ALWAYS CLEAN YOUR BRUSHES AND ROLLERS

If I could afford a 'Roller' then I'm sure that I could afford to pay somebody to clean it for me! Seriously though, it's very important that you purchase good quality brushes and rollers – the quality will be reflected in the standard of the finish you achieve. And make sure that you clean your tools thoroughly when you've finished. Just like any other tools, brushes and rollers need to be 'broken in', and they will improve with use. As a matter of fact, a good quality range of brushes and rollers should last a lifetime for an average family. And remember, if you get your brush out and it feels a little stiff, just run a wire brush over it – that will soon soften the little blighter up!

TYPES OF PAINT

The range of paints and finishes now available seems vast. In fact, it's not as complicated as it first appears, provided you know the effect you want and the base of the paint you're using. Generally speaking, water-based paints are faster drying and easier to clear up, but they may not be as hard-wearing as their oil-based equivalent. So, when you're choosing what type to use, remember to consider how much wear-and-tear the surface is likely to receive.

TYPE OF PAINT	USAGE	FINISH	NOTES	CLEANING
OIL-BASED				
Primer	Wood/metal	Flat	Use this to seal bare wood	White spirit
Undercoat	Wood/metal/plaster	Semi-flat	Apply this as a base for the top coat	White spirit
Gloss	Wood/metal/plastic	High sheen	Hardwearing and durable	White spirit
Eggshell	Woodwork	Satin	Hardwearing and durable	White spirit
WATER-BASED				
Primer	Wood/metal	Flat	Only use on interior woodwork	Water and soap
Undercoat	Wood/metal/plaster	Semi-flat	Apply before water-based top coat	Water and soap
Satin Finish	Wood/metal/plaster	Mid-sheen	Quick and relatively durable	Water and soap
Eggshell	Wood/metal/plaster	Mid-sheen	Top coat for interior work	Water and soap
Vinyl Matt Emulsion	Plaster	Flat	General purpose coverage	Water and soap
Vinyl Silk Emulsion	Plaster	Mid-sheen	General purpose coverage	Water and soap
OTHERS				
Varnish	Woodwork	Various	Available as water or oil-based in a variety of finishes	Check label
Wood stain	Woodwork	Matt/silk	See above	Check label
Knotting fluid	Woodwork	Matt/silk	Used to seal knots in wood prior to painting, varnishing or staining	White spirit
Paints for Metals	There are a number of paints available, but by far the best paint to use is a Hammerite-type paint especially designed for finishing metal.			White spirit

BASIC CHECKS

When taking possession of a property, either by purchasing or renting it, make sure that you locate and inspect all of the main services in case of emergencies. It's a bit like taking a first aid course for people. In fact, that's quite a good analogy, because you will be carrying out first aid on your property and to do that successfully, you need to know where and how the vital organs work.

So, get your torch and ladder out, pick up your trusty pad of paper and pen and start jotting down exactly where all your meters, stopcocks, fuseboards and boiler controls are to be found. This might seem like a drag – and it's probably the last thing you will want to do having just moved in – but believe me, you won't regret it when you have your first blown fuse, burst pipe or exploding boiler!

One of the most potentially damaging disasters that can occur in a property is a burst or damaged water pipe. Unnoticed, it can cause a huge amount of damage and inconvenience, particularly in the winter, when the pipes are subjected to the extremes of the cold weather. The problems will often occur when the occupants are away on holiday, even for a couple of days, and prevention rather than cure is the obvious answer. So turn off the water supply when you go away! This means that you must locate the water supply stopcock.

For a house, there is normally a stopcock in the front garden near the boundary or outside the property boundary in the street. This stopcock is the property of the water authority and any leaks occurring on the property side of the stopcock are your responsibility. The stopcock can usually be accessed by a turnkey,

which can be acquired from a plumber's or builder's merchant. Turning off from here will automatically cut the supply to your house.

Houses and flats normally have a stopcock inside the building close to the first call on the supply. This will typically be the kitchen sink for the fresh drinking water and the stopcock is commonly positioned under the sink or nearby [A]. Turning off this stopcock will isolate the incoming supply. A water supply normally diverts after the kitchen sink and feeds a storage tank in the loft or cupboard, which in turn supplies the bath, WC and hand basin with the coldwater supply. This water is not for drinking.

The supply feed pipe to the tank also has a stopcock to enable you to isolate the supply to the bathroom area without

stopping the freshwater supply to your kitchen sink.

In an emergency, shut off all stopcocks and empty the water storage tank by turning on the bath and hand basin cold taps and repeatedly flushing the toilet. This will empty the system down the drains as opposed to all over your house!

While we're on the subject, check whether your water pipes and storage tank are lagged [B]. It's a small investment and could save you a small fortune and a lot of heartache. (See pp. 48–9.)

The second power source you need to locate is the mains gas shut off valve [C]. The valve is normally located on the incoming supply just before the meter as a rule. It has just a quarter turn off and on. Again, the valve is normally located in a cupboard under the stairs or in a high position on a common area such as a landing. In recent years the gas supply companies have been fitting the supply meters and valves to an outside box. This is often the case in properties that have been split into flats.

Next on the list is finding out what type of boiler system you have. A family house or larger would normally have a conventional system, which incorporates a gas boiler [D] and copper cylinder [E] (see overleaf). In a smaller property, a gas combination boiler system is commonly used, which will only heat the water as you require it without a cylinder storage system. Read the instructions on how to start the boiler and how to operate the timer switches.

IMPORTANT NOTICE

If you smell gas, do not try to fix things yourself! Do not turn on any lights or electrical appliances. Turn off the gas supply by the valve and exit the property ensuring everybody else has left as well. Telephone the gas company's emergency telephone number to get them to come and check out the fault immediately.

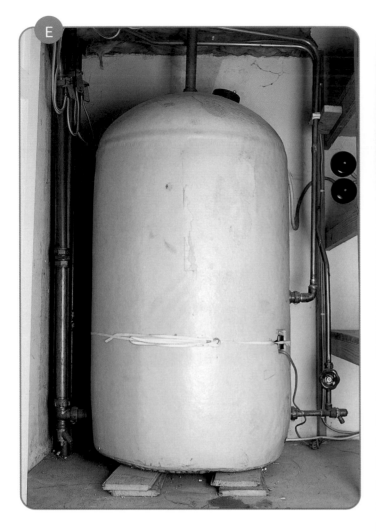

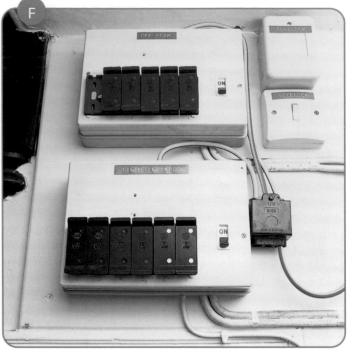

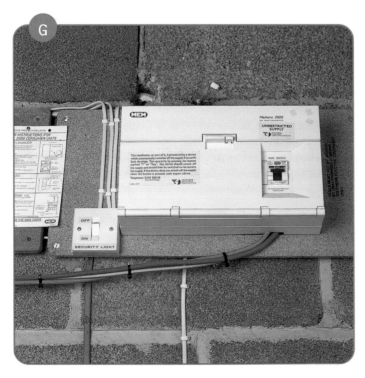

You should have a written record next to the boiler indicating when the previous services were made and when future services are required. Servicing of the appliance is very important to ensure that the boiler is running correctly and that no toxic emissions are returning into the property. Make sure that ANY gas work undertaken in your property, is carried out by a CORGI-registered contractor – and check his credentials.

Another vital organ to locate is the electricity supply fuse board, called a consumer unit [F]. The consumer unit can be positioned in a cupboard, possibly under the stairs, or high up by the front door, and controls the electrical supply to your home [G]. Inspect the unit and check what type of fuses it contains to see whether they are fuse wire or cartridges, and make sure you have some spares close at hand. I always keep a torch, electrical screwdriver and a pack of assorted fuse wire next to the consumer unit, as well as candles and matches as back up in case I've forgotten to change the batteries in the torch!

Keep a list of important emergency numbers to hand of various tradesmen [H]. If possible, have the contact details of at least two of each – your careful organisation and planning could fall apart if the plumber you've got noted down decides to go off on holiday to the Tropics in the week you get a leak. And above all, make sure your systems are serviced regularly – prevention is always better (not to say cheaper and much less stressful) than cure!

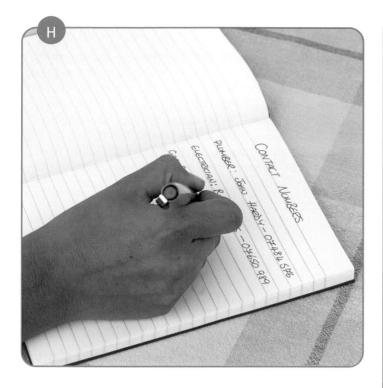

TURNING OFF THE POWER

In emergencies, you should know how to switch off the supply of electricity to the entire house. On the consumer unit you will see a main isolating switch – if ever in any doubt, flick this switch. Similarly, before you start any electrical work around the home, flick this switch. You should then remove the miniature circuit breaker (MCB) or individual circuit fuse, which will cut off the power supply to the relevant circuit on which you wish to work. When the job is done, replace the MCB or circuit fuse and put the power back on. NEVER take short cuts when dealing with electricity.

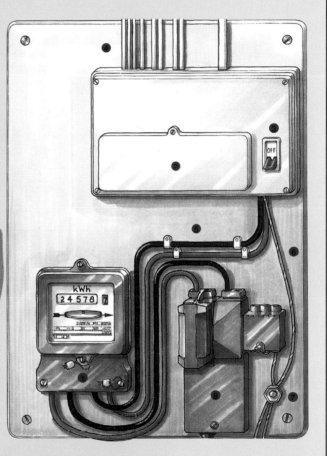

Typical fuse-board layout. **1** Meter; **2** Consumer unit; **3** Main isolating switch; **4** Power and light-circuit cables; **5** Meter leads; **6** Earth cable; **7** Consumer's earth terminal; **8** Service head (also known as the cutout)

TOMMY'S TIP

Build up a relationship with recommended tradesmen by having them call to check out and service your systems before you have to call them out in an emergency. They will advise you of any alterations you should consider.

Avoid being forced to call out an emergency tradesman without them having any previous working relationship with you, as this service tends to be much more expensive. Try to remember, prevention, not cure, is the solution.

PLANNING

When everything seems to be going wrong, you will discover that with honest analysis, the problems are inevitably caused by a lack of planning. Now, I'm not saying that unforeseen circumstances don't play a part, but in every walk of life a simple bit of planning may enable us to avoid the common pitfalls.

You will find that this is particularly true when it comes to DIY. I always say to people that when you wake up on a Saturday morning determined to redecorate the lounge that weekend – STOP. Put the kettle on, make yourself a nice cup of tea and sit down with a pencil and pad of paper. It is so important not to rush into things – especially when time is limited – because nine times out of ten you will make a botch of the job and wish you had never started it in the first place. Far better to take your time, be realistic about how much time you have available and take it nice and slowly.

It is essential to plan the operation carefully. Write everything down to be sure [A]. Firstly, do you cover the carpets with sheets or do you roll them up? If you can, roll them up. No matter how careful you are, you're bound to knock over a can of paint or bucket of paste, so decant the contents of larger containers into smaller ones to reduce the likelihood of mishaps [B]. Are you stripping the paper from the walls? You can hire or even buy a wallpaper steam stripper; it's a great investment for anyone! Then there's sanding down the woodwork, painting the ceiling, painting the woodwork, the list goes on. Why try to do it all in a weekend? Prepare and strip the walls one weekend, then purchase the materials and complete the job the following weekend. Your project will be pleasant and rewarding and feel a lot less like a chore! That's the key! Because you have the time, you can clean and store all your equipment properly instead of hastily sticking the brushes in an old can of water only to find they are hard and ruined the following week.

FIRST AID

If you plan your DIY jobs properly and always take your time, with a bit of luck you won't be needing a first aid kit. However, there is an element of risk with many jobs, and it is just as well to be prepared, so I recommend that you keep a good basic kit to hand in case of emergencies. In addition to the items listed below, make sure you've also got some good old fashioned iodine – a bit fierce but invaluable nonetheless – some antiseptic cream and some eyewash, which is essential. Oh, and some headache and indigestion tablets are also a good idea... You can buy ready-made up kits in most DIY stores, chemists or department stores, and remember to replace items if and when you use them.

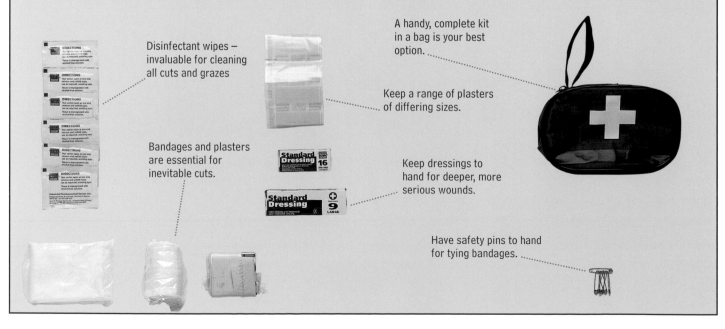

Disinfectant wipes – invaluable for cleaning all cuts and grazes

A handy, complete kit in a bag is your best option.

Keep a range of plasters of differing sizes.

Bandages and plasters are essential for inevitable cuts.

Keep dressings to hand for deeper, more serious wounds.

Have safety pins to hand for tying bandages.

If you plan the project to coincide with taking the family out for a meal, or better still, a romantic meal for two, you can finish the day's work at a reasonable time to allow for clearing up. You will be ready for a fresh start on day two.

Where possible, always try to carry out DIY tasks in daylight hours. Use the evenings for planning and get an early start on the job. The hours between 7am and midday are worth twice as much as the hours between noon and 6pm with regards to what you can achieve.

If you are sanding down furniture or moveable objects, try to do it outside. If that's not possible, or you are sanding floors, seal the door up with masking tape and polythene then cover with a dustsheet. Open the windows and wear a mask. Also try to bear in mind that your neighbours might not want to listen to DIY noise all day, so call and tell them what you intend to do and remember to finish at a reasonable hour.

In your planning stage, always make sure that you allow for protective coverings and cleaning equipment such as: dustsheets; polythene; heavy duty rubbish bags; cleaning rags; brush and pan; mop and bucket; disinfectant and air fresheners. Also, have to hand a first aid kit (see opposite), and, most importantly, don't forget to include all the health and safety gear that you will need. As my Dad would always say to me, 'Son, if a job's worth doing, then its worth doing properly!'

TOMMY'S TIP

Never leave the cleaning up until the next day. If you think removing day-old grease from the washing up is hard, try removing stripped wallpaper that has dried and stuck to the floorboards. Remember to clean as you go along.

MENDING A FUSE & FITTING A PLUG

You've spent all day preparing for a wonderful dinner party, or maybe Mum's calling around to see how you're settling in. You're confidently cooking a spaghetti bolognaise, with fifteen minutes to go, then – disaster! All the lights go off and you discover that the power has gone off as well....

One of the first things you should do when taking possession of any new property is to locate the position of the fuse board (or 'consumer unit'). Check out the type of fuse board you have and familiarize yourself with the unit. The fuse board is basically a safety valve for the power and lighting circuits in your property and controls a series of ring mains, normally comprising two rings for each floor – one for lighting and one for power. The fuses should be clearly marked on the inside of the fuse board cover – 5 amp fuses for lighting circuits and 15 amp fuses for power circuits.

I'll show you how to fit a plug as well, whilst we are at it.

Locate the position of your fuse board, using a torch if necessary. Ensure that the master switch is in the OFF position and then find the individual fuse that needs its wire replacing.

Tools Required:

Torch
Electrical screwdriver
Wire cutters
Ordinary screwdriver

Here's a very useful piece of information – always keep a torch, spare batteries, fuse wire, candles and matches as back-up in an accessible location close to the fuse board.

MENDING A FUSE

Using your torch, check the fuse board master switch is in the OFF position. This will probably already be the case, as when a fuse blows, normally it will automatically throw the master switch to the OFF position. To locate the blown fuse, remove the fuses one at a time and inspect the thin fuse wire to make sure the wire is unbroken. On the card of fuse wire, select the appropriate amp fuse wire to match the blown fuse. Using a small screwdriver, carefully unscrew the two screws a little way at either end of the fuse. Remove the damaged remains of the old fuse wire and carefully thread the new wire through the centre porcelain part of the fuse. Wind the wire around the first screw then the second and tighten down the screws, snipping off any excess wire.

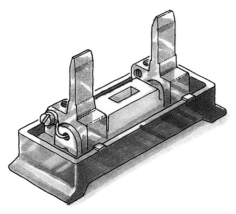

This is an old-fashioned single-bladed carrier with a wire fuse. It features a thin wire running from one contact at each end to the other.

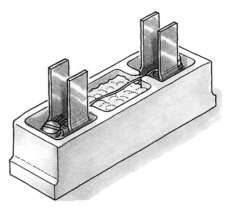

This is a double-bladed carrier with a wire fuse. It works in the same way as the single-bladed carrier.

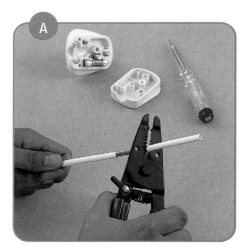

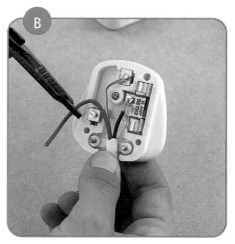

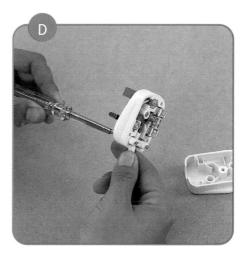

Replace the repaired fuse and then the fuse board cover. Throw the master switch to the ON position.

FITTING A PLUG

Open up the plug case with a screwdriver and use wire strippers to remove the outer casing from each of the wires in the cable [A]. Use the ends of the wire cutters or a pair of pliers to position the exposed copper ends of each coloured wires in the correct terminals – brown to live, yellow and green to earth and blue to neutral [B].

Holding the wires carefully in place in the terminals, drive the terminal screws tightly down on top of the wires using a screwdriver [C]. Ensure that no loose bits of wire protrude from the terminals. Finally, tighten up the screws securing the cable grip [D], replace the plug cover and switch on.

TOMMY'S TIP

Use flat wire cutters to strip the cable and wire covers before you fit the plug. Don't forget to turn the power off first, though!

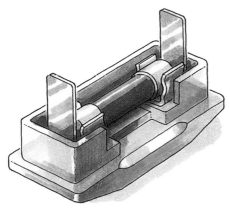

These days, many fuses are the much easier to change cartridge click-and-fit type, with no fiddly fuse wires to cut and wind.

CHANGING A SOCKET

My first house was terribly dilapidated and contained only six single power points throughout. The whole electricity supply was ancient and needed to be completely renewed. Anxious as I was to get the job done, I installed lots of power points, mostly on one side of the house, but these were badly planned. They ended up being positioned in all the wrong places. It's lucky I have eyes in the back of my head so that I could watch the telly!

Before you start, it's a good idea to plan where you think your furniture and appliances are going to be located around the room in question so that you can ensure that the power points are installed within easy reach. You may find (like I did), that you need to move the socket from behind the sofa, or you want an extra power point without having to use an extension cable; these pages explain how you can do these things with minimum fuss.

Tools Required:
(some optional, depending on type of wall)

Small electrician's screwdriver
Medium screwdriver
Wire strippers
Drill
Masonry drill bit
Clubhammer
Small bolster or cold chisel
Padsaw

Single power points are not much cheaper than doubles, so when fixing a new socket you might just as well fix a double.

The power supply is simply a continuous cable loop of 2.5mm twin and earth (three cores; two sheathed – live and neutral, one unsheathed – earth), pulled through where the power points are located, then looped on to the next point and so on. This is called a ring main. There is one on each floor of a house for power and a separate ring for lighting.

CHANGING FROM A SINGLE TO A DOUBLE POWER POINT

Turn OFF the power from the mains. Unscrew the retaining screws on the single socket face and pull the face out to reveal the cables [A]. Unscrew the wires and remove the socket face. Disconnect the interior of the single socket box and remove the back box by hand [B].

If the power point is mounted in a plasterboard partition wall, mark the outline of the box on to the wall with a pencil and, using a padsaw, cut out the piece of plasterboard [C]. Fix the new plasterboard back box, pulling the cables through to the front of the box [D]. The wiring will be the same for a single or double socket outlets – two red wires (live), two

TOMMY'S TIP
Use an electrical wire detector to check the exact positions of wires in walls before you begin drilling or hammering.

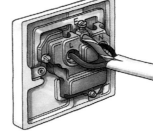
This diagram shows the correct wiring for a single socket outlet – red to 'L' for 'Live', black to 'N' for 'Neutral' and green and white to 'E' for 'Earth'.

Connecting a socket to a ring circuit. The wiring procedure is basically the same. Bend each stiff conductor until it folds into the mounting box.

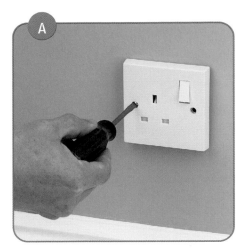

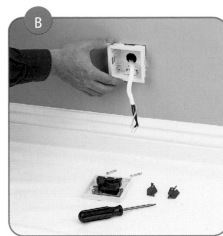

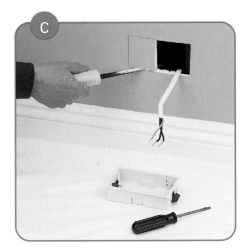

black (neutral) and two green and yellow (earth). Connect up the wires accordingly [E], replace the double socket cover and secure the screws [F].

If the power point is mounted in a solid wall, position the new double back box and mark the wall with a pencil. Remove the existing single socket box.

Using a masonry bit and drill, create a series of holes following your pencil line to the depth of the new back box. Then, use the clubhammer and small bolster or cold chisel to break out the rest of the plaster and brickwork around the drilled holes.

Place the new double socket box in the new opening, mark two of the fixing holes. Using plugs and screws drill the holes, pull the cables through and fix the back-box in position, ensuring that it is flush with the plaster line. Finally, make good the edges of the opening around the box with filler and smooth with sandpaper.

TO ADD A POWER POINT TO THE EXISTING RING MAIN

In order to add a new power point to the existing ring main, locate and fix the new power point box as described, also cutting a chase in the plaster to bury the new cable below the box, and let into the floor void.

Turn OFF the power from the mains and test the existing socket switch with an appliance before removing the socket face. (See previous instructions.)

Strip back the ends of the new wires and add these to the existing wires – black to black (N), red to red (L), yellow and green (E) – then fix the socket face back in place.

Run the new wire under the floor from the existing socket to the new socket. Strip the wire ends and fix to the new socket outlet. Make good the changes with plaster or filler and sandpaper smooth when dry.

CHANGING A LIGHT BULB HOLDER

Isn't it strange how when you get a toothache, it's always over the weekend when all the dentist's surgeries are closed, and you wind up spending all evening in a hospital A & E with a student dentist practising on your molars.

In the cold light of day and in differing circumstances it might not seem a very wise decision to let a novice loose inside your laughing equipment. But as I remember so well, at that stage, if the prognosis was 'off with the head' I would have willingly agreed!

What has the dentist got to do with a light bulb holder? Problems always seem to occur with lighting at night when it's dark. OK, that's fairly obvious because that's when you use the lights! My point is, if possible, leave fixing them until the morning when you can turn off the power and actually see what you're doing. Not only will the job be much easier in daylight – it will also be much safer!

Here's a sequence of events which leads to a common problem in many households. The bulb to the central light in your living room blows and you decide to replace it. As you are replacing the bulb, the bulb holder crumbles and the new bulb pops out again. Suddenly, the simple job of changing a lightbulb becomes a daunting DIY task – or does it?!

CHANGING A BULB

There are basically two types of bulb or light fittings – a (threaded) screw-in type and the more common double pronged, push and twist (bayonet) type. You should know what type of bulb you need – including the wattage – and always keep spares to hand.

Changing a light bulb is a simple task and it can be replaced without turning off the main power at the fuseboard. Make sure that the light switch is in the OFF position before you start. However, if the bulb holder is faulty, then you must TURN OFF the power from the mains fuseboard before you do anything.

Position your steps under the light (do NOT use a chair) and assemble the replacement bulb holder and tools required on the platform. Undo the threaded plastic ring to release the lampshade and put it aside.

REMOVING THE OLD BULB HOLDER

Before doing anything, turn the power off! Then unscrew the top section of the bulb holder [A] to expose the two connecting wires. These wires will be held in place by two grub screws. Undo the two screws [B] to release the wires and remove the damaged bulb holder. The top part of the bulb holder will then slide down over the wires to complete the removal process.

The ends of the wires often become brittle from the heat of the bulb over a long period of time, so cut off the last inch (25mm) of flex. Then use the wire strippers (see page 23) to strip back the wire casing a further $^1/_2$ inch (12mm) [C] before you fit the new bulb holder.

Sometimes, very old bulb holders can be difficult to unscrew. This is usually because engrained dirt has got into the plastic threads. A little lubrication will normally solve the problem.

Tools Required:

Stepladders
A small neon electric screwdriver
A pair of wire strippers
Sticky tape

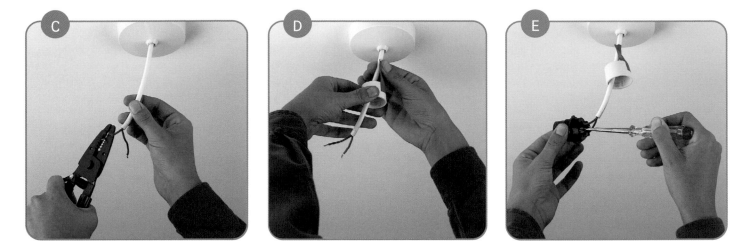

FITTING THE NEW BULB HOLDER

Unscrew the top section of the new bulb holder and slide this over the wires. Then, use a strip of tape [D] to hold the top section of the holder in place and stop it from sliding down, until you have connected the wires to the main body of the new bulb holder.

Undo the grub screws of the new bulb holder, insert the wires and tighten the grub screws one at a time ⌊E⌋. It doesn't matter which side you put the wires into a bulb holder! Loop them over the supporting lugs to prevent the weight from being carried to the terminals and to reduce stress on the unit as a whole.

Remove the tape to release the top part of the bulb holder, and carefully screw it onto the main body. Then unscrew the plastic retaining ring which holds the lampshade in place, and insert the shade [F].

Carefully screw the retaining ring back on (taking care not to cross-thread), to hold the lampshade in position [G]. Finally, insert your new bulb, and turn the power back on.

If you have any problems getting the new bulb holder to work properly, chances are that either the bulb has blown or the wiring is not properly secured. Check both and proceed as before until you get a result.

TOMMY'S TIP

Use a soft cloth or teatowel when removing a bulb that's just blown, as they can get tremendously hot.

FITTING A DECORATIVE CEILING ROSE

As a child I remember the beautiful ceiling rose and cornice work in the living room of our terraced Victorian house. I used to lie on the floor on my back gazing up at it for ages, making different shapes and faces in it. I used to do the same thing at the park looking up at the clouds in the sky. If it appears that I spent long periods of my childhood lying on my back, I've certainly had to make up for it, as I've got older.

Whether or not it's because of my childhood surroundings that my favourite period of construction is Victorian I'll never know, but it certainly was a period of exquisite ceiling decoration. Some were subtly understated whilst others were wildly flamboyant. The cornice is decorative ornate plasterwork created to disguise the join between the walls and the ceiling. The ceiling rose was designed to enhance the beautiful central light (often a chandelier) and made to match the detail of the cornice. Victorians in particular designed their cornice work to appear more on the ceiling and less on the wall.

Now I'm not suggesting that you be a Victorian, but a plain ceiling can look extremely spartan. That doesn't mean there isn't a place for the modern look too, but why not take up the challenge and fit a modern style ceiling rose – it doesn't even have to be made of plaster. But, I must admit, I still have a hankering after those Victorian ceiling roses!

There are plenty of plaster ceiling roses to choose from. Plastic and polystyrene types are also widely available from DIY stores and good decorating shops. But if you want something special, you will have to go to a fibrous plaster specialist. As you all know, size IS important!

You may well manage to fix a small or medium-sized ceiling rose on your own or with the help of a partner, but for a large 'all singing and dancing' one, I suggest you get all your friends round, or leave it to the experts.

FITTING A NEW CEILING ROSE

Assuming you have no central light in place, the first thing to do is find the centre of the ceiling. This is achieved by using two lines of string each stretched diagonally from corner to corner of the ceiling [A]. The point where the strings cross each other will be the centre [B]. Where there is already a light fitting, remember to turn the power supply OFF and remove the fitting first. Make sure you have set up a safe platform to work from.

Offer up the new ceiling rose (also centred) and draw around the edge with a pencil onto the ceiling [C].

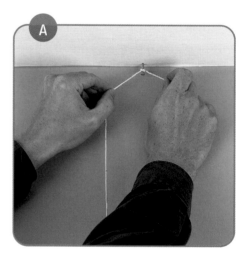

Tools Required:

New ceiling rose
Tacks
String
Pencil
Straight edge
Joist detector
Drill
PVA adhesive
Brass screws
Screwdriver
Filler

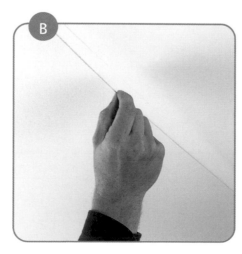

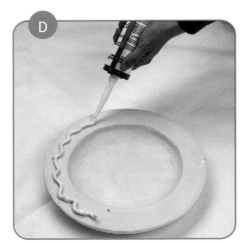

For a lightweight rose such as the one shown in the photographs, apply a coat of PVA adhesive and water to both the ceiling (remove any ceiling paper first) and the back of the rose to seal the surfaces [D]. Apply plaster or tile adhesive to the back of the rose and press into place [E]. Wipe off any excess plaster or adhesive [F]. Have someone hold the rose in place and then pull the lighting flex through the centre of the rose. Use wire strippers to cut back the cable and strip the wires ready for wiring into the light fitting [G]. Fill over any screwheads with filler and leave to dry. Paint to finish.

If you are attaching a heavy rose, use a joist detector to locate the joists within the proximity of the rose (see my tip, right). Take the straight edge and pencil and draw two centre lines on the ceiling and transfer corresponding lines onto the rose. Carefully drill two pilot holes, then a light countersink and have two long brass screws ready for fixing (see artwork below).

TOMMY'S TIP
Use a joist detector before doing any drilling work into ceilings, floors or walls. It's a great tool that could save you a fortune!

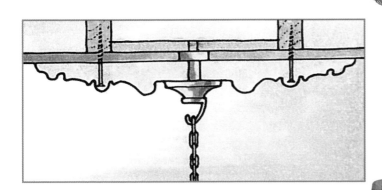

Above: For a larger, reinforced moulding it is generally necessary to drill holes into the ceiling joists and attach the moulding with screws rather than using adhesive.

FITTING A SPOTLIGHT TRACK

Replacing a standard pendant light fitting with a spotlight track system can create a very satisfying transformation without breaking the bank.

These track systems are available in a variety of different designs and finishes, so they are suitable for different locations within the home – from the hallway to the lounge, and most popularly in the kitchen and/or dining room. The track system gives you the flexibility to position individual lights along the track to pick out specific areas or features for highlighting, such as a stylish cooker in the kitchen or maybe favourite pictures on the wall in the living room. For example, if there is a particular shortage of natural light in the corner of a room, a cleverly positioned spotlight can make all the difference and bring that area to life.

The connecting blocks of track systems are commonly positioned at one end of the track, so bear this in mind when making your choice, as it will affect where in the room you are able to locate the spotlights. There are also some tracks with the connection block situated in the middle of the track, which may save you having to make alterations to the lighting circuit.

Before you start, turn OFF the power. Unscrew the cover of the existing ceiling rose by hand [A] and then disconnect the wires from the terminals with an ordinary screwdriver [B]. Next, unscrew the base of the rose from the ceiling [C]. Assuming you have access to the floor above, lift the floorboard directly above the ceiling rose and replace the existing rose for a junction box located between the floorboards and the ceiling. Try to fix the track to some of the floor joists if you can.

Mark drilling points with a pencil [D], drill holes and press in rawlplugs to receive the screws that will hold up the base of the track [E]. Alternatively, fix some battens above in the ceiling void to take the track fittings. Screw the base of the track to the joists or battens [F], and then pull any excess flex into the ceiling void. Follow the instructions supplied with the track.

Tools Required:

Measuring tape
Electrical screwdriver
Hammer
Insulating tape
Nail bar
Ordinary screwdriver
Drill and pilot bit
Wire strippers

TOMMY'S TIP

Use an electrician's screwdriver to detect live current when working with power.

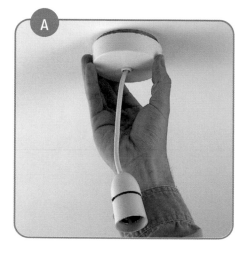

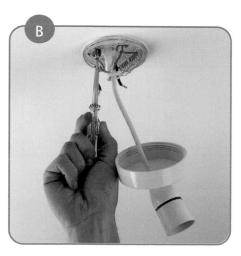

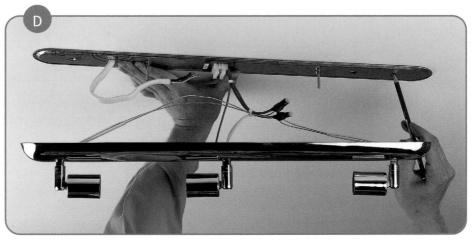

Wire one end of the length of flex into the junction box and the other end into the track connections [G]. Attach the cover of the spotlight track [H] and switch the power back on.

Ceiling fixings and instructions are normally supplied with all spotlight track systems. Remember to check that the number of lights you want to use will not overload the lighting circuit – the shop selling you the spotlight track should normally be able to advise you on this.

As a general rule, if you are in any doubt about performing an electrical task such as this one, don't do it – get a qualified electrician to come in instead. Electricity is one area of home DIY that you really cannot afford to mess around with....

LOW VOLTAGE LIGHTING

Commonly known as 'downlighters', low voltage lighting systems provide an attractive feature but may be too complex to fit for the amateur. However, there is a new, simpler low voltage system available without transformers, which are actually contained within the lamps.

Check with your supplier whether conditions within your property are suitable for the installation of downlighters.

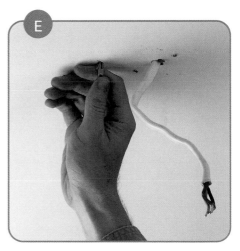

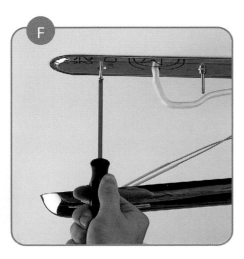

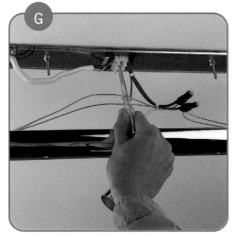

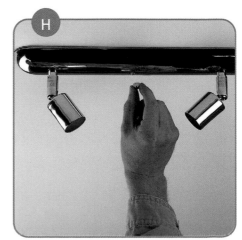

FITTING WALL LIGHTS

Don't make the mistake I made if you want to fit wall lights in your home. Select and fit your wall lights BEFORE you finish decorating and have had your carpets fitted. Although my wife and I planned our house refurbishment carefully, we found that when the curtains were fitted in our lounge they reduced the natural light considerably. The two main lights made the room too bright and we required something a touch more subtle – controlled backlighting. So up came the bedroom carpets upstairs, and out came the hammer and bolster chisel for our lovely decorated lounge walls. So

remember, we ALL make mistakes! One good thing that came out of that experience was that we knew exactly where we wanted to put the wall lights because of the position of the furniture.

As a guide for when marking out the position of your wall lights, it's best that you locate them centrally in each section of wall. This task is not as difficult to attempt as it sounds – just follow the process through the various steps detailed below. All you have to do now is decide where in your room you want to situate the lights!

Tools Required:

Tape measure
Pencil
Spirit level or chalk line
Sharp bolster chisel
1kg (2lb) club hammer
25mm (1in) cold chisel
Paintbrush
PVA adhesive
Plastering trowel
Wide bladed scraper
or filling knife
Electrical screwdriver
Hammer
Drill
Masonry bit and plugs
Wire strippers

CUTTING THE CHASE

Mark the position of the wall lights, and using a spirit level and pencil, draw two vertical lines approx 40mm (1½in) wide up to the ceiling. Cut along the lines using a 1kg (2lb) club hammer and narrow bolster chisel. Using a cold chisel and hammer, cut back the plaster chase [A]. Normally the plaster is thick enough to house the cable, but it is good practice to house the cable in conduit or plastic capping to protect it. This may mean cutting the chase a little bit deeper to accommodate the conduit. Fixing the conduit or capping can be achieved by using 40mm (1½in) galvanized clout (plasterboard) nails knocked into the mortar joints [B]. Plaster over the conduit to a smooth finish [C] (see my tip, right). The cable you should use is 1mm² twin and earth type. Fit the light switch and cable up to the junction box, and loop the cable in and out for each wall light mounting position, finishing the cable run at the last of the wall light mounting positions.

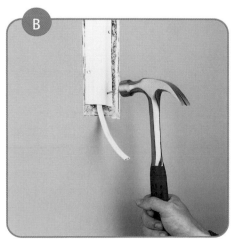

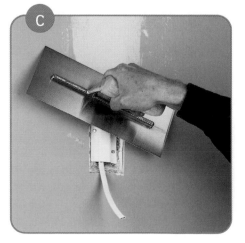

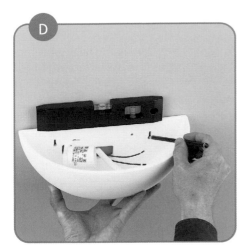

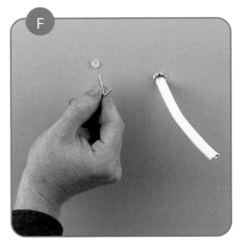

Cut back the ends of the conductors (wires), fixing the two red conductors into one terminal and the two black conductors into the second terminal. The earth wire should be sleeved and connected to the mounting box.

FITTING THE WALL LIGHT

Mark the fixing position of the wall lights on the wall with a spirit level and pencil [D]. Drill fixing holes into the wall for all the light fittings [E], insert rawlplugs and screw in hooks by hand for securing the units to the wall [F]. Offer up the wall light units, push the cable ends through the holes in the back and secure them to the wall [G]. Cut back the conductors 12mm ('/₂in) and fix the brown conductor into the other end of the red terminal and the blue conductor into the other end of the black terminal [H]. The power should be turned OFF to make the final connection with the lighting ring main into the new junction box.

TOMMY'S TIP

For a perfect finish, fill the chases with bonding plaster. Before the plaster sets completely, use a scraper carefully to cut back each edge to allow for the finish plaster, which is applied to give a flush and smooth finish. (A rub over with sandpaper and block ensures a completely flawless finish.) Finally, paint the lights the same colour as the walls so they match perfectly.

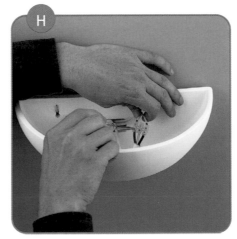

CURING A DRIPPING TAP

For some reason we always tend to leave a dripping tap for ages before repairing it. This could result in bad staining to the sink or hand basin or, worse still if you are on a water meter, an extra cost to your bill. But whatever the reason, leaving a tap unmended is a terrible waste of water. I do tend to 'create' in my house if I find somebody hasn't turned a tap off properly – it's such a waste of a precious resource! My bedroom is right next to the bathroom and a dripping tap is like Chinese water torture. I cannot abide a ticking clock in the bedroom, so a dripping tap is anathema to me.

Tools Required:

Slotted screwdriver
Small adjustable spanner

TOMMY'S TIP

You can use silicone grease as a lubricant to help ease any stiff washers off or onto the tap's innards. Also, it is a good idea to soak the new washers thoroughly in hot water to make them more pliable and easier to fit. Always keep a supply of washers to hand.

There may be a few different reasons for a dripping tap, but all are fairly simple to solve. Mixer taps on the kitchen sink are very commonplace today, so this is the kind of tap you are most likely to encounter.

Before you begin, remember to turn OFF the water supply. If the tap is leaking from the base of the spout, remove the spout [A], prise off the circlip at its base and check the washer at the base of the spout for wear and tear [B]. Replace the washer if necessary.

Next, prise off the head cover of the tap itself [C]. You will need to remove the shrouded head from the tap to expose the retaining screw. If there is no screw, the head will just pull off, exposing the spindle [D]. Use an adjustable spanner to remove the spindle headgear [E]. Then remove the spindle itself [F].

There are normally two O-rings, which when worn leak water from the top of the tap shroud. There is also a rubber tap washer at the bottom of the headgear, held on with a nut. Undo and replace this washer [G] if the tap is dripping from the spout.

There are more O-ring seals on a swivel spout. If water seeps out on the swivel, these O-ring seals need replacing.

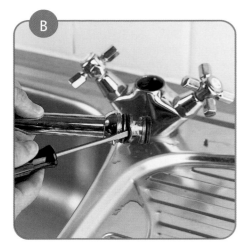

Undo the small grub screw and pop out the swivel spout and replace the seals.

If the headgear is all seized up and corroded, purchase a headgear replacement kit. Take the tap headgear with you when you buy any replacements. Go to a plumber's merchant to get expert advice, because the manufacturers make different size O-rings and washers. Of course, wouldn't it make everything far too simple if all the products were standardized!

If you have ceramic disc taps, then these are supposed to be maintenance-free, but problems can still occur. There is nothing in plumbing that is entirely without trouble! Even though there are no washers to replace on ceramic disc taps, if they need repairing you will have to renew the inner cartridge as a whole. To remove the headgear from the tap body, take a spanner and turn it anti-clockwise. If there's any muck on the ceramic discs, clean it off and refit. If the

tap still leaks, off to the shop you go! Take the tap innards with you as they are 'handed' – cold is right and hot is left – and it is vital that you get the right components for each one. If the seal on the bottom of the cartridge is worn, replace it. Basically, inspect all the parts of the tap carefully when you have dismantled it: you might as well fix any and all faults at once.

I know there is quite a lot to think about in all this, but whatever you do DON'T forget to turn off the water from the main stopcock and open the tap to drain water from the pipe before you do anything else. If it's a bathroom tap that needs fixing – that is, one that runs from the cold water storage tank and not direct from the rising main – you will either need to shut off the stopcock from the tank or drain off the tank by opening all the taps in the bathroom. Oh and finally, a really handy little tip: before beginning work, always replace the plug so that small objects don't fall down the plughole!

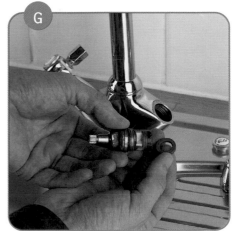

CHANGING THE TAPS ON A BATH

If you want to smarten up an old bath or sink, a good way to do this is to change the taps to a new set. The effect of the transformation can be amazing, especially if you redecorate the bathroom at the same time. If the enamelling on the bath is sound, a good clean will bring back the sparkle. Limescale and chemical cleaners are available for stubborn stain removal. If that doesn't work, specialist companies can re-enamel your existing bath. This is definitely not a DIY job, but if you want a tip as to how to complete the job really effectively, replace the waste and overflow on the bath, or have the existing one re-coated.

If you have an old pair of taps or mixer unit, consider restoration as an option, particularly with period properties and vintage sanitary ware, which is often worth keeping.

Think carefully about what you are going to buy as replacement bath fittings, because the choice available is absolutely vast. Personally, I have always steered clear of coloured sanitary ware. It can date very quickly and if you want to change the bathroom decor it can be restrictive. I believe you can't beat a white bathroom suite, whether modern or period style, with chrome fittings for easy cleaning and non-tarnishing.

Butler kitchen sinks have enjoyed a renaissance in recent times and look superb with a great set of mixer taps, regardless of whether the sink and taps are renovated originals or reproductions. Even the bog-standard stainless steel sink will benefit from a change of taps.

CHANGING A TAP

Turn off the isolator valve (if you have one) with a slotted screwdriver [A]; otherwise, turn off your mains stopcock and drain down the system by opening the taps.

Undo the pipe work and waste connections beneath the bath or sink's taps [B]. Unscrew the back nut using a wrench [C] and lift out the old taps [D]. This is a good opportunity to

Tools Required:

Slotted screwdriver
Wrench

clean the area thoroughly around the taps before refitting the new taps or mixer unit.

Insert the new taps or mixer into position onto plastic or rubber washers to protect the sink and seal from leaks [E], press the unit firmly home [F], and then connect the pipes to the base of the taps beneath the bath [G]. The distance between the centres of tap holes on sinks and baths is generally between 175–180mm (7–7$\frac{1}{4}$in). There are swivel union attachments that can be added to allow a lot more tolerance.

Make sure you fit the flat rubber washer and hand-tighten the shower hose [H], if there is one. If you want to give the hose a half turn with the wrench, use a cloth to avoid any scratching.

Take this opportunity to fit some flexible copper pipe to the tap tails to enable easier fitting and maintenance – this will mean some small adjustments to the pipe work.

The procedure for a sink mixer is as above, but you might be able to remove the sink for ease of fitting as you change the taps.

TOMMY'S TIP
It is worth investing in a plumber's pipe-cutting tool if you are going to do a lot of DIY on your waterworks.

CHANGING A WASHER ON YOUR BALLCOCK

I have very vivid memories of changing the washer on my own water tank ballcock. It was a chilly autumn evening, the sun was setting and dusk was rapidly approaching. The overflow pipe from the cold water storage tank in the loft had been running all day, discharging water in the area where my wife normally hangs the washing out. I had just got in from a hard day's toil, but to please my wife I went up into the loft with a bag of tools and a torch.

This took place many years ago, and it has to be said I was a touch impetuous and didn't prepare properly for the task in hand. I didn't bother to set up a board in the loft to work from and was merely balancing on the joists. Now, you can guess what happened next! Not only did I slip through the ceiling, I fell through with both legs on either side of the joist! As I say, vivid, but also very painful memories, and it looked for a while as if a complete new ballcock would be required!

So... be warned! First set up a working platform, and if you don't have permanent lighting in your loft, set up a running lead light and attach it to the rafters so that your hands are free.

CHANGING THE WASHER ON A WATER TANK

Shut off the water supply to the loft storage tank (see artwork left) by turning off the stopcock. Then drain off the tank water by opening the bathroom taps. Take out the split pin from the valve, which will in turn release the float arm. Unscrew the cap at the end of the float valve, pop out the piston from the body and unscrew the piston end cap. Stop the piston rotating by inserting a slotted screwdriver into the gap. Remove all the remains of the old washer and clean the cap out with a wire wool pad and fit in the new washer. Lubricate the new washer with a touch of silicone grease. Connect the float arm to the valve, re-fix the split pin and turn the water back on.

The more recent systems have adopted the diaphragm valve system, which basically replaces the washer with a

The cold-water storage tank, or cistern, supplies the hot-water cylinder and all the cold taps in the house, other than the one in the kitchen that is used for drinking water.
1 Float valve; 2 Reinforcing plate; 3 Tap connector; 4 Rising main;
5 Tank connector; 6 Gate valve; 7 Distribution pipe – 22mm (³/₄in);
8 Pipe clip; 9 Overflow-pipe assembly; 10 Overflow pipe; 11 Vent pipe

Tools Required:

Plumber's grips
Bradawl
Slotted screwdriver
Wire wool pad
Silicone grease

large rubber diaphragm. The idea behind it is that it is less likely to wear and it is made of plastic. Replacing the diaphragm is based on the same principle as the Portsmouth valve (nicknamed the navy valve) and the older Croydon valve (nicknamed the airforce valve). If you are not sure which valves you have or how they work, try the information box (right) or ask at your local plumbing supplies store.

CHANGING THE WASHER ON A TOILET

To turn off the water supply to the toilet cistern, without interfering with the supply to the rest of the house, use a slotted screwdriver to turn the isolator valve screw [A]. Once this is done, drain down the cistern by flushing the toilet.

Undo the top of the valve with the arm and float connected and set aside [B]. Next, unscrew the ball valve assembly and remove the plastic piston [C].

Remove the old washer, ensuring that any remaining residue around the washer is carefully removed, using the pad of wire wool [D]. Fit the new washer and lubricate it with a touch of silicone grease.

Fit all the components of the cistern back together again, turn the water back on and try flushing the loo. Hopefully, everything will work properly and you should be flush with your own success! If not, take everything apart once more and try the whole procedure again. If that doesn't work, call a plumber!

HOW VALVES WORK

The Portsmouth valve has a solid brass rod float arm with either a copper or plastic float attached to the end. Bending the rod downwards slightly forces the float down and cuts off the valve earlier, letting less water into the tank. Bending the rod upwards opens the valve longer and allows more water into the tank. On a diaphragm valve, there is a screw on the float arm, which when turned towards the valve, lowers the water level, or when turned away allows more water into the tank.

TOMMY'S TIP

You will find it easier to use modern push-fit fittings for plumbing jobs like this one. They are far less trouble to handle than the more fiddly conventional metal plumbing fittings.

CLEARING BLOCKED DRAINS AND TOILETS

Drains! Drains are things that people generally don't like to think about until they really have to... Drains are where all that muck and rubbish and dirty water disappear into.

Sticking to a few simple rules and occasional maintenance duties should ensure a continual uninterrupted effluent flow, into the mysterious underground depths below. However, unless you're a very sensible person, initially you'll probably make the same mistakes I made when I moved into my first property. There I was, making a nice big breakfast in the morning, happily tipping the fat from the pan down the sink on top of the bolognaise waste from the night before. Nobody told me what I should (or shouldn't) do! It wasn't long before I was in deep trouble – everything above ground was blocked and it was such a pain to clear!

To clear the kitchen sink, try a spoonful or two of caustic soda first [A], and if that doesn't work, use a plunger. Place a cloth in the overflow then pump the plunger up and down over the waste outlet [B]. Repeat the process until the blockage clears. If the blockage remains, you should undo the trap under the sink [C], and try clearing that.

If the toilet isn't flushing away properly, this would suggest that a blockage has already formed. Deal with this problem immediately, or you could have the WC overflowing into your bathroom! Not a pleasant event...

Now, I was taught a very handy way of clearing a simple blockage in the WC bowl, when a youngster has thrown something in and blocked it up. Take a black rubbish bag, roll your sleeves right up and put your arm into the bag right to the bottom. Lower your bag-wrapped arm into the loo and grab the offending object. As you withdraw your arm, allow the bag to close itself around the item. Obstruction removed, arm dry, and you don't have to see the offending article if you don't wish to!

There is also a larger version of the kitchen plunger available for hire for clearing toilets, which you push down into the bend and pump. If this works, the water level will drop quickly and the WC will make a belch-like gurgling sound. Rinse with hot water and disinfectant to clean.

Hire a WC auger if the blockage is still solid [D]. This is a flexible cable, which should be pushed as far as possible into the bend [E], with the handle then being cranked to unblock the loo. Again, when you have finished, rinse with hot water and disinfect.

Before you start any of the major internal operations explained above, my advice would be to lift up the manhole cover in the garden or street if possible, to check whether or not that is blocked.

Hire a set of drain rods, or borrow a set from Great Uncle Bertie. Screw two rods together with a plunger or corkscrew top at the head [F]; slide this into the drain run, going with

Tools Required:

Plunger
Auger
Wire coat hanger
Protective clothing
Disinfectant and soap

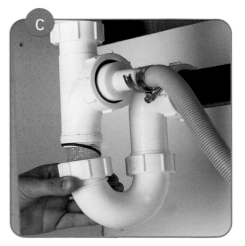

the flow of the waste water. Add another rod each time it becomes necessary and push the assembled line of rods to and fro, further into the drain [G]. It helps if you have a hose running into the manhole to help flush the blockage through.

If the manhole is not blocked, it may be that the soil stack pipe is blocked. Undo a rodding eye on the stack using a hired auger to clear the blockage.

Blocked gullies are easily cleared. Raise the grille and put your hand into the gully (wear rubber gloves) and remove any debris from the trap [H]. Ensure the outlet from the gully is also clear. Rinse the gully with the hose and clean with suitable cleaner.

I should know how to clear a drain, because my father declared one of the funniest moments of his life was when we had to clear some blocked drains on a long curved drain run. I was at the bottom end and Dad was up the top end. The manhole covers were off and Dad was rodding away and he shouted over to me 'Can you see anything?' Well, I was young and naïve, and didn't consider my Dad could be so wicked.

'Inappropriate timing' springs to mind as I bent down to look into the manhole at that particular moment. Dad had just freed the blockage as he called out to me. I heard a noise but realized the impending disaster just a tad too late! Ten tonnes of you know what hit the bend of my manhole at once, and I had just opened my big mouth to say...! I never did get to finish that sentence. In fact, I never even got started on that sentence, but I have to say, it ranks as one of the worst moments of my life, especially when I stood up looking for help only to see Dad and the lads laughing their heads off....

TOMMY'S TIP
Put a bowl under the waste before you undo it, rather than after as I did, to avoid smelly, dirty water pouring inside your lovely new units!

CLEARING AIRLOCKS

Air locks are a common occurrence in heating systems and are fairly simple to cure. Air locks in the plumbing system, however, may be a little more complex to solve.

There are two main possibilities when air locks occur in the hot water supply. Firstly, your plumber may have been an aspiring Picasso who decided to create a piece of modern art that could be nominated for the Turner Prize. Let me explain by pointing out that some plumbers (not particularly good ones), choose to take the easy option and go around objects rather than through them, hence creating a problem with too many bends! This can cause air pockets and resultant problems, which would take a skilled amateur or a professional to sort out.

The other more common cause is too great a demand on the reservoir (water tank) system in your home. You're filling the bath for a lovely soak, running the hot and cold water taps at the same time. This is a double demand on the water tank supply, as the cold tap is fed directly from the tank and the hot water cylinder is also fed from the tank. Somebody's using the loo (that's fed from the tank); the washing machine is switched on, fed from the cold mains slowing the supply to the tank. The hot feed to the washing machine is fed from the cylinder, also supplied from the tank. Now somebody's doing the washing up, more demand on the mains cold supply which means even less water to the tank, and the hot supply is from the cylinder – even more demand from the tank! Get the picture?

Now, as if all that wasn't enough, Grandad has decided to water the garden – even more demand on the mains – so practically nothing is left to feed the tank. The water level in the tank gets so low that it drops below the outlet pipe, thus allowing air into the system. These circumstances may seem exceptional, but in today's society they are actually quite common – the demand for water is constantly growing! (I haven't even mentioned the dishwasher, washing the car, or anyone taking a shower!)

When an airlock occurs, it normally appears as a spluttering and hissing tap. The air needs to be forced out, so to solve the problem, you'd best start at the first port of call (so to speak), the kitchen sink. Take a piece of rubber hose – slip one end over the spout of the kitchen mixer tap [A], and the other end over the spout of the bathroom basin hot tap [B]. Turn the cold tap on the kitchen mixer tap wide open [C], then turn the hot tap on the basin wide open [D], which will force the air through the bathroom hot tap by using mains pressure until the water is flowing freely.

To clear the bath taps, repeat this process by closing the basin tap, and if necessary the tank supply, by closing the

Tools Required:

Piece of rubber hose
Radiator valve key
Dry cloth

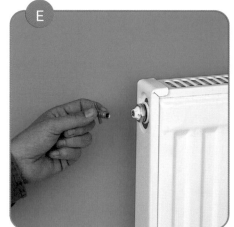

TOMMY'S TIP

If you have an airlock in your heating system, first try the humble radiator key to bleed all your radiators. More often than not, this will do the trick.

hand basin hot tap, forcing the air bubbles into the tank. The whole line is now clear.

If you have a mixer tap in the kitchen, remove the spout and hold your hand tightly over the opening. Fully open the hot tap and slowly open the cold and force the air up through the open bath tap.

Another common cause is if the water mains supply is turned off and the tank is emptied. This will allow air into the system. The remedial process is the same as described above.

Air trapped in a radiator is easily detected by touch. If only half the radiator is hot, you probably have an air pocket trapped within the radiator, which will affect its efficiency. There is a small bleed valve on the top left or right corner of the radiator. You will need a radiator key to open this valve (these are widely and cheaply available from plumber's merchants or DIY stores). Push the radiator bleeding key onto the valve [E] and turn it gently to release the trapped air (you will hear a hissing sound), until water begins to squirt out. When this happens, immediately shut off the bleed valve. Be prepared, and have some old rags on hand to soak up any spillage [F].

Check the water pressure indicator on your combi boiler. (Your boiler should display information on the panel regarding the level of pressure required.) If the pressure is low and needs topping up, carefully open up the screw on the valve in the filling loop at the bottom of the boiler[G], using a slotted screwdriver if necessary. Watch the water pressure indicator and shut off the feed immediately by turning back the valve screw when the correct pressure has been reached.

FITTING THERMOSTATIC VALVES

In this age of striving for better use of energy, in an attempt to reduce greenhouse gases and save a nice few quid at the same time, try fitting thermostatic valves to your radiators, replacing the standard rad valves. This gives you much more control over the temperature. It's not necessary to fit thermostatic valves on all of the radiators, just in particular hot spots or hot rooms – the kitchen for example, which may already be hot. A thermostatic rad valve allows you to turn down the radiator temperature for that room alone without affecting other areas in the property. Used in conjunction with a room thermostat and an automatic timer, if you make a conscious effort, you can create an efficient heat control system, thereby saving money and helping out the ozone layer!

Tools Required:

Adjustable spanner
Plumber's grips/wrench
Radiator valve spanner
Pipe cutter
Dry cloths

TOMMY'S TIP

When removing the standard valve to replace it with the thermostatic valve, keep and use the blue cap supplied with the latter. If you subsequently remove the radiator, you can tighten this cap onto the remaining section of the valve to avoid explosive accidents like the one described opposite!

Drain down the system by firstly shutting down the boiler. Leave for a while to allow the water to cool, and then switch off the supply to the expansion tank via the stopcock. Next, slip one end of a length of garden hose over the drain cock, the other end into the gully. Open the drain cock with a key or adjustable spanner and release all the water. Any water trapped can be removed by opening the bleed valves on all the radiators, starting at the furthest from the drain cock. Pack some dry cloths around the pipe under the old valve. Hold the main body of the valve with a set of grips and, using an adjustable spanner, undo the radiator union nut [A]. Apply the same method removing the cap nut from the bottom of the valve [B]. Carefully lift off the old valve [C].

Removing the cap nut and olive could be tricky. If the olive is brass (yellowish) it can be removed with care, freeing the cap nut [D]. A copper olive (same colour as pipe) would have compressed onto the pipe when tightened so requires cutting the olive off with pipe cutters. Some thermostatic valves may be longer or shorter than the original, requiring some alteration to the pipe work.

Slide on the cap nut and then the new olive [E]. Older valves might have different tails from new thermostatic valves, so it is

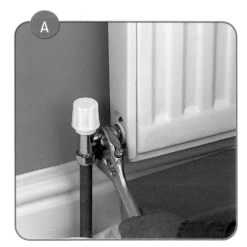

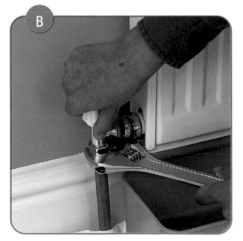

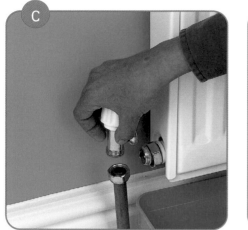

important to compare the originals with the tail supplied with the new valve. If they are different, fit the new tail into the radiator by using a rad valve spanner (a large Alan key).

Don't forget to wrap PTFE tape around the thread half a dozen times or so before fitting. Half-tighten the valve to the union first, then the cap nut [F]. Once aligned, tighten the union first, then finish tightening the cap nut [G].

Originally, thermostatic valves had to be fitted on the radiator flow side (ingoing) but now modern thermostatic valves are bi-directional, which means, I suppose, that the water can flow both ways through the valve (that is, the valve can be fitted on either side of the radiator).

A CAUTIONARY TALE

I must tell you a story concerning thermostatic rad valves that happened to me, which was a disaster in itself, but could have been a horrific disaster. We were renovating a large four-storey early Victorian listed building and had meticulously restored two beautiful period ceilings. We were at the decorating stage and more than half finished, so the job was nearly completed. We left work as normal on Friday evening and by complete chance I happened to be driving by the building on Saturday morning. It was a bright and sunny December day but very cold, so imagine my horror when I spotted smoke coming from the third floor window. I stopped the car and saw water pouring through the brickwork. I thought the fire brigade must be inside, but where was the fire engine? I opened the front door and found I was in a sauna! You couldn't see for the steam and water. The beautifully restored ceilings in the reception rooms had water pouring through – hot water, at that!

I ran up to the next floor and there was the culprit – water and steam spouting from the thermostatic valve! Let me explain. We had removed the radiators to re-decorate properly, which is a perfectly safe thing to do with a thermostatic rad valve, except that in extreme drops of temperature, the water can circumvent the O-ring inside the valve and create what appears to be a hot water geyser – in the middle of your house! When you purchase a thermostatic rad valve, you will find a small blue plastic cap inside the box. In the event that you may remove the radiator, you just have to tighten this cap onto the remaining section of the valve, so avoiding the almost coronary-causing disaster that befell me.

INSULATING/LAGGING TANKS AND PIPES

Pipe and tank insulation is a useful task to perform – it insulates hot water pipes and tanks, keeps the water hot and saves a fortune in heating costs. On cold water pipes and tanks, it works in the opposite way, keeping the cold out and thus preventing burst pipes or leaks in the winter months.

Believe me, it could save you thousands of pounds and lots of grief for less than a hundred, and a bit of effort. I have seen the results of many burst pipes, which have caused devastation for the property owner and could have easily been avoided for a modest outlay.

TOMMY'S TIP

Always insulate the actual pipes whenever you can. Modern pipe lagging is relatively cheap, widely available and easy to fit. It will save you a fortune in bills in the long run.

Tools Required:

Craft knife
Sharp kitchen knife
Saw
Paint brush
Adjustable square

LAGGING A COLD WATER TANK

To lag a cold water tank, the easiest method is to buy a purpose made 'insulation jacket', which is fibre glass wadding inside a plastic covering which normally has its own fixing ties. Fixing it to the tank is usually pretty straightforward and self-explanatory.

If you do not wish to purchase a ready-made insulation jacket, it is possible to make your own by cutting pieces of hardboard to match all four sides of the tank (as well as its lid). Cut some roof insulation and stick it to the hardboard by painting PVA adhesive on with a brush and placing the insulating material directly on top of the glue. Alternatively, you could just place a cut-down piece of insulating material in a black plastic sack and make a blanket that way [A].

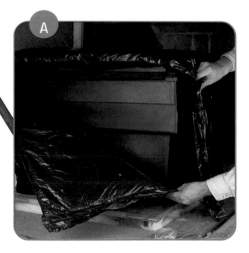

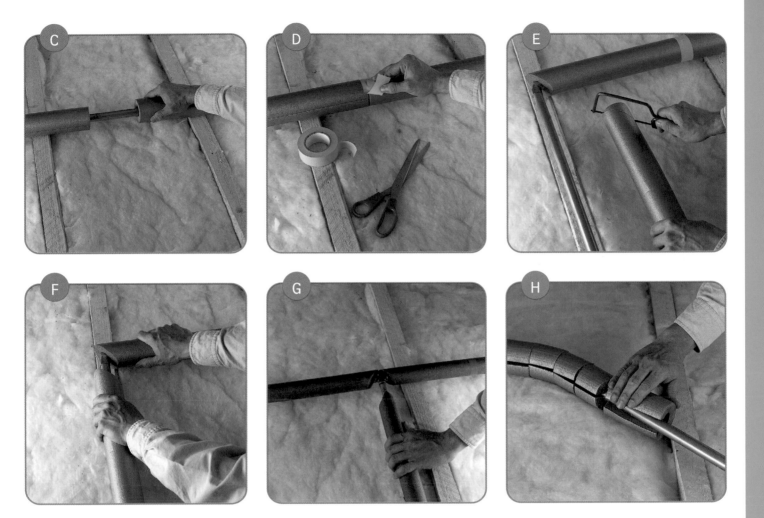

Secure the panels or blankets in place around the tank with string [B]. It may not look pretty, but it will stop the big freeze!

Whenever you are working in the loft, ensure that you place a short scaffold board or similar across the joists, to avoid accidents and damage to the ceilings – always remember safe practice!

INSULATING PIPEWORK

Pipe insulation is very simple to fit. There is a felt-sock type of material on a roll that you slide over the pipe, normally fitted when the pipes are actually being installed in the first place, and more often used under floors and screeds, or the foam type, which comes in long lengths and is usually pre-split along its length for easy installation. The latter is much better for fitting to pipes which are already in position.

Cut the tubes to length with a craft knife. Open the tube by the split and pop on over the pipe [C]. Abut straight joints and use insulating tape to seal the joints [D].

A right or left hand bend requires a mitre cut. Using an adjustable square, mark the 45° angle and cut the tube to length. Repeat the process in the other direction to complete the angle [E], press the two angled ends of the insulating material together to make the joint [F], and tape the join with insulating tape.

To make a tee joint, cut a 90°-angled cut to half-depth on a straight length of insulating sock, and then cut a matching shape to fit snugly against this [G]. Complete the joint by taping the pieces together with insulating tape.

Insulating around a bend in the pipe work is achieved by cutting a series of V-shaped cuts on the one side of the tube, bending it to the shape of the bend as you squeeze the tube onto the pipe [H], and then sealing the cuts and joints with insulating tape in order to hold all the pieces firmly in place.

INSULATING LOFTS

The first loft that I ever insulated was our family home – the memory of which will stay with me forever! My dad had a really wicked sense of humour, forever playing games and having a wind up. I was very young and naïve and I believed and trusted everything he said.

Dad had applied for a loft insulation grant, which was available at the time, and asked me to insulate the loft. The rolls of glass fibre were delivered and I went up to fix it (bearing in mind that I was only about fourteen years old and getting paid about £10, which was a lot of money then). Because it was midsummer, dad said it would be boiling in the loft as we had a slate roof, which really soaked up the heat. He also said it would be dirty (he was right there!), so I decided to do the job dressed only in shorts and boots.

At the time this seemed like one of my better, bright ideas, because of the intense heat in the loft. It was also much easier to move around the loft unencumbered by overalls and so on. If like me at the time, you have never worked with fibreglass before, you may be forgiven for not understanding what happened next, but my dad – he knew what I was in for!

If I were to run a tyranny, the best form of torture I could impose (other than forcing someone to read a love scene from one of Alan Titchmarsh's novels), would be to strip them naked and rub fibreglass wadding all over their body. I was itching and scratching for two tortuous days and nearly tore my skin off. Dad, as usual, thought the whole thing hilarious but denied any responsibility!

The moral of the story is twofold: one, don't necessarily believe everything your dad tells you; and two, if you want to insulate your loft, do the job in cold weather and cover yourself up with layers of clothes – overalls, gloves, hats, goggles, masks, the lot – so there are absolutely no gaps!

There are two main types of insulation – blanket (in rolls) or loose fill (in bags). The most common form of insulation is the blanket type. The recommended minimum depth of insulation is 150mm (6in), but the more the merrier – remember 25 to 30 per cent of heat loss occurs through un-insulated roofs.

Prepare for the job properly and work off a couple of short scaffold boards laid across the joists. If you don't have a permanent light in your loft, use a lead light hung up at a high vantage point. Bring all the insulation into the loft space but don't open any of the rolls until you are actually ready to fit out the loft. When packed, the insulation is compressed, so when it's rolled out between the joists, it will expand a bit. The rolls are approximately 39–41cm (15–16in) wide x 7.5m (25ft) long. Trim the ends in a chamfer shape to allow airflow from the eaves, then begin rolling out the insulation blanket [A]. Try to ensure that electrical cables aren't covered by the insulation. Lift the cables and roll the insulation underneath [B]. This will avoid any overheating of the cables. Also ensure that any light casings or lamp fittings protruding into the loft are not covered. Trim closely around these with an extended craft knife or sharp kitchen knife [C]. Beware of cutting any cables! To make doubly sure none of the heat escapes from your property, lay a second layer of insulation at right angles to the first and cover right over the joists [D]. The procedure is the same as that for the first layer, as are the precautions.

If you are using loose fill insulation, it is very important to cut strips of plywood or hardboard fixed between the joists to form a barrier and keep the eaves clear [E]. The depth of fill

Tools Required:

Handsaw
Measuring tape
Short timber batten
(straight edge)
Craft knife or
kitchen knife
Lead light
Protective clothing
Mask
Goggles, etc.

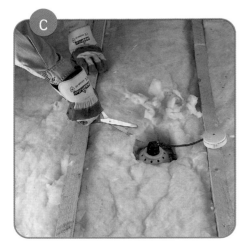

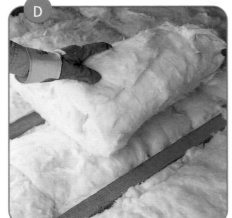

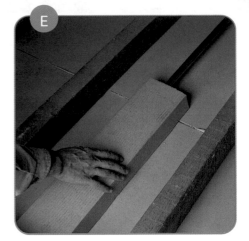

necessary is approximately 15cm (6in) – you may need to raise the height of the joists by attaching battens, thus allowing boarding to be laid down for walking on in your loft.

Pour in the insulation fill [F] and spread with a timber or plywood off-cut. Tamp down and level the insulation fill so that it lies evenly between the joists [G].

To help prevent cold water pipes freezing in the winter, create a bridge out of hardboard before filling with loose fill insulation. This will allow warm air from below to circulate around the cold water pipes. Saw strips of hardboard to length with a handsaw. Using a craft knife and straight edge, cut a pair of parallel lines to the pipes on the hardboard and snap only halfway through, thus forming a bridge to lay over the pipes.

TOMMY'S TIP

If you are working up in the loft, don't take any chances. Look where you are walking (or crawling!), only ever putting your weight onto joists, and balance carefully at all times. Ideally, before you start, build yourself a platform from plywood or planks of wood across the joists to sit or kneel upon as you work.

INSTALLING A LOFT LADDER

I have to admit I have a confession to make. People constantly say to my wife how lucky she is to be married to me! My wife would question all and any aspect of that statement! People then qualify the statement by saying it must be amazing to have someone who can make all those things and do all those jobs.

To be fair to myself, I'm normally reliable when it comes to fixing things, although I do wait until there are half a dozen things, and fix them all at once. I will, however, have to put my hands up on this occasion. I have been meaning to fit a loft ladder to my loft for a long time (it's too embarrassing to say how long), but suffice to say that the step ladder parked on the landing will no longer do! I shall have to fit one!

Loft ladders are a very clever and efficient way of making use of normally inaccessible and unused space, particularly in inner city and urban areas where space is often at a premium. We all have to reconsider how we use any space available to us in a practical and constructive way. Even if only used for storage, loft space is ideal, and a fitted loft ladder will enable the space to be used safely and effectively.

Loft ladders are normally made to suit three different ceiling heights – 2.3m (7ft 7in), 2.5m (8ft 3in) and 2.9–3m (9ft 6in–10ft). They normally operate on a slide and fold basis, or are the concertina type. Some loft ladders even incorporate a handrail. The type I am fixing in the illustrations on these pages is a slide type. It may not be exactly the same make as your own chosen ladder but the principle is the same, and each ladder should carry its own fitting instructions.

The loft trapdoor must be hinged to open downwards, so the hinges provided must be fixed to the same side of the opening as the loft ladder [A]. The trapdoor should be made from 19mm ($^3/_4$in) plywood, MDF or blockboard and must be fitted flush with the ceiling.

Lower the ladder to the floor. Engage the catches and make sure they are locked in position. Fit the loft ladder guide assembly to the frame with the screws provided [B] and [C]. Make sure that the climbing angle is correct by checking the special angle indicator on the side of the ladder. Slide down

Tools Required:

Screwdriver
Drill
Pilot bit
Tape measure
Handsaw

TOMMY'S TIP

Make sure that your loft ladder is fully extended and locked-out before climbing it. Otherwise, accidents can happen all too easily. You may find, like me, that **not** having a loft ladder makes access to your storage area very difficult indeed!

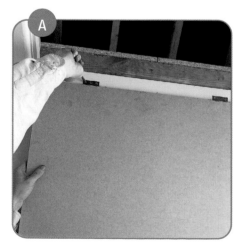

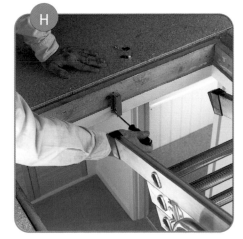

the two plastic stops to the top of the guide assembly and tighten all four screws [D]. This will ensure that the ladder is always in the correct position for climbing into the loft.

Fix the pivot arm to the floor of the loft [E]. Close the three sections together, making sure the catches lock in position, and push the ladder up fully into the loft. Slide the 2 plastic stops up to the underside of the guide assembly and tighten the four screws [F]. This ensures the ladder clears the trapdoor when closed. Attach the handrails to either side of the middle or top section [G].

To fix the automatic latch, position the latch in the centre of the frame surround and opposite the trapdoor hinges [H]. The latch must be set back by the thickness of the trapdoor.

Engage the pointed marker into the latch and close the trap door. Where the point marks the trap door, is the position for fixing the striking plate. Test the position by opening and closing the trapdoor until you're happy with the smooth operation [I].

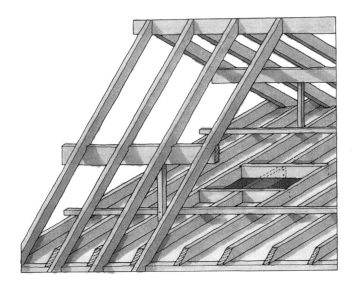

This diagram shows the construction of a typical loft hatch opening, demonstrating the necessary positions of joists and trimmers. A loft hatch must never be positioned so that it undermines the strength of the ceiling.

REPLACING/REPAIRING DAMAGED FLOORBOARDS

Just as fashions in dress come and go in cycles, the same can be said for styles and trends in property and furnishings. The last few years have seen a slow but steady change from 'must-have' fitted carpets to expensive hardwood and cheaper laminate floors. However, by far the most popular choice is to use the existing original floorboards, which would normally have mellowed nicely in colour and should have done most of the shrinking that they are going to do.

There are some very important factors you should be aware of before you venture down this route.

Firstly, and probably most importantly, if you are choosing to expose your groundfloor boards, do remember that almost all wooden (board type) floors are suspended floors. This means that the floorboards are fixed (generally nailed) to a supporting framework of timber joists, which are in turn supported and suspended from the ground by small brick walls. Very importantly, these floors have air vents to the front and rear of the property to allow unhindered air circulation, which prevents infestation by woodworm, wet and dry rot, and so on.

Over a period of time as the sap in the floorboards dries out, the boards tend to shrink and gaps form in between the boards. In the winter it can be too much to bear with northerly winds whistling up your trouser legs! You may also find that you are constantly dusting the furniture as well. Floors on the upper levels are not normally affected in this way because they are closed-in floors and no ventilation is necessary.

If your property has had central heating fitted or been rewired or both, when you take up the carpets you might well find that the floorboards are a bit of a shambles. Most plumbers and electricians are motivated by speed to finish the job, so they tend to pay little respect to floorboards, particularly if they would appear to be hidden by other floor coverings. They rip up the boards cutting the wood where convenient, to suit themselves (often cutting two boards on the same joint), and breaking pieces off when lifting the boards.

Although this is really not a major problem under carpets, it certainly will be, once the boards are exposed!

REMOVING DAMAGED FLOORBOARDS

Carefully remove the skirtings that are fitted around the area of floorboards to be replaced or repaired. (Refer to Replacing Skirtings, pages 64–5.) This will allow easier lifting of the boards.

Removing the first board is the most difficult. Carefully insert the nail bars on opposite sides of the board and central to the length (if necessary tap with a claw hammer) and lever the board upwards [A]. Use wooden blocks for extra leverage – this will also help to prevent damage to the adjacent boards [B].

Repeat this process along the length of the wood. Starting at the middle will help spring each board away from the joists. Once the first board is removed, access is easier for the removal of all the others, using exactly the same technique.

Tools Required:

Cordless drill
2 flat-type nail bars
Claw hammer
Pinchers
Cramps
Wood chisel
Tenon saw
Hand saw
Electric sander
PVA wood glue
Pins
Floor brads

REPAIRING AND REPLACING BOARDS

You can cut out any damaged sections in a square form to simplify a replacement. Carefully mark the board around the damaged section using a square [C]. Use two wooden battens to keep the rogue board supported above the floor, allowing the damaged section to be cut out using a tenon saw [D].

Mark and cut a matching piece from another board. Cut the replacement section 2mm ($\frac{1}{8}$in) oversize, to ensure a tight fit with no gaps. Use a wooden block and hammer to tap the replacement section into position. Nail the new board in place [E]. Smooth with a sander or by hand using sandpaper and a block.

To replace boards, remove all the old nails from the joists using the nail bars and claw hammer [F]. Drill fine pilot holes in your new boards to prevent splitting and to locate and direct the position of the fixings [G]. Stagger the cut boards to avoid two joints abutting side by side. Secure with floor brad nails [H].

TOMMY'S TIP

For any nails left in the floorboard, pull through from the underside to prevent breakout to the face of the board. Also, carefully mark new boards with a pencil or crayon to indicate any pipe runs and so avoid puncturing when refitting.

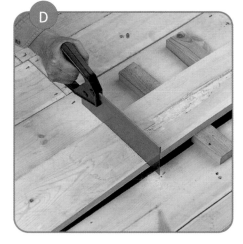

SANDING FLOORS

A finished polished floor really does look the bee's knees, but getting to that stage is not always as simple as it seems! I will endeavour to explain how, and give you a few tips on what to do and what not to do! But I must tell you about my first experience with sanding wooden floors.

The whole ground floor of our present house is laid in wooden block flooring, made from Douglas Fir, in a herring bone pattern with straight borders. It was covered in manky old carpets when we first looked at the house. I sneaked a peak underneath and saw the floor. Well, that swung it for me; we just had to buy the house.

A friend of my father's, a local school caretaker named Vince, told me he used to sand and seal the floors for the school on a regular basis, so I enlisted him for the job. I cleared the ground floor of furniture completely and hired a drum floor sander. Vince started sanding and I went off to buy the lacquer. I was only gone for an hour, but when I returned, I couldn't find Vince for the dust. I followed the sound of the sander and found him! He was completely covered in dust. I asked why he hadn't emptied the dust bag on the machine to avoid all the mess. Bless him! The sweat was pumping out of him and he said, 'I couldn't turn the damned thing off!' When the dust had settled a bit, I was able to inspect what he'd done. I ate the head off him! He had started sanding with a coarse paper, and because he couldn't stop, he had cut into the block floor over half an inch deep! Vince said, 'It was like using a lawn mower!'. I replied, 'With the tramlines you've cut into it, it looks just like Wembley!'

Vince, bless him, decided that he would stain the wood down a bit to match the panelling, before he lacquered the floor. Golden Oak was the colour he chose without consulting us. When I returned, it looked like the black hole of Calcutta and I had to sand the whole floor down again myself!

Needless to say, Vince was last seen running towards the Emerald Isle being chased by an angry housewife wielding a large kitchen knife!

After the initial shock, my wife and I were able to see the funny side and every time we look at the floor in that room we have a good laugh.

Wooden flooring has steadily increased in popularity – both solid and laminate-type floors. Normal laminate floors cannot be sanded down, because the surface is only a few millimetres thick of formica, and below that is the sub-strata of MDF or chipboard. Sanding and lacquering the old original floorboards is particularly popular. It's noisy, dusty, messy and hard work, but it can be very rewarding.

The first job is to inspect the condition of the floorboards. Tap down the floorboard fixing nails with a suitable nail punch [A] and remove any other nails or screws. All this will help to avoid tearing the sanding belts.

If woodworm has attacked the floor, lift the boards carefully, treat the joists and the back and front of the contaminated boards, and then re-fix. To sand and lacquer over the woodworm gives the floor 'character'. If the woodworm is too severe or a board is damaged, cut it down in length or scarf in a repair using wood glue and pins or a clamp. Any repairs or replacements should be done using the same boards! Replacements can be taken from elsewhere in the house or from a reclamation yard. New boards just will not match (and look terrible into the bargain!).

Lay the floor drum sander on its back (unplugged); undo the retaining bar and fix the sanding belt [B]; screw it down

Tools Required:

Drum floor sander
Edging sander
Hook scraper
Corner sander
Claw hammer
Pinchers
Screwdriver
Nail punch

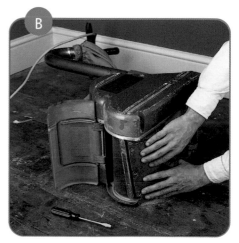

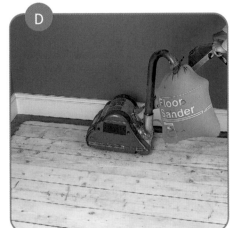

tightly to avoid the belt coming loose. There are three grades of sandpaper – coarse, medium and fine. Unless the boards are very rough, you may only need the medium and fine.

If the boards have cupped (curled), this can be tackled by running the belt sander across the room at 45° [C] and again at 45° from the other angle. When the floor is perfectly flat, use a fine belt and sand along the board length and grain [D].

Hire an edging sander to sand the edges where the drum sander is unable to reach. The pads are fitted to the machine by a central bolt on the underside [E]. Avoid overrunning this machine on the floor [F], otherwise you may make swirl scratches. Use the hook scraper for difficult tight areas or corners [G].

Dust the area thoroughly. Now wipe the floor over with a cloth and white spirit, ready for the lacquer. You will need at least two coats of lacquer, but for a better finish apply more coats. Always apply lacquer with the grain of the wood – never across it [H].

FIXING A LAMINATE FLOOR

Wooden floors are the 'in thing' at the moment, but they are not new by any means! What is new however, is the laminate floor. Popular demand for a wooden floor at a cheap price has led manufacturers to develop a flooring from a sub-strata (either MDF or condensed chipboard) approximately 8–9mm (³/₈in) thick with a 2mm (¹/₈in) thick veneer surface which gives the appearance of a very hard wooden finish.

Wooden floors have long been admired and sought after, but have always been the preserve of the relatively affluent because of their expense. Laminate flooring has brought wooden floors to the masses. They are a highly popular choice – and I think in some ways a healthier choice than fitted carpets. It's easier to clean a laminate floor and it doesn't play host to dust mites, which are particularly problematic to people who suffer from asthma, allergies or bronchial problems. The disadvantages are that they are not as warm and cosy as carpets. Carpets are also soft underfoot.

The boards generally come in 2 metre (6ft 6in) lengths, tongued and grooved all around, and because it is only about 10mm (¹/₂in) thick, it's ideal for covering an existing floor. Laminate flooring is available from DIY stores and most builder's merchants. It's very reasonably priced, from only £8.00 per metre, which allows it to compete very favourably with fitted carpets.

Firstly, repair any damage to the existing floor and screw down any loose boards. (Check for pipes before fixing down any loose boards. Use a pilot drill and countersink bit to guide the screws.)

TOMMY'S TIP

I prefer to remove the skirtings before fixing laminate floors. However, before you do this, use a 15mm (⁵/₈in) block and pencil to mark the skirtings all the way round. Follow the procedure described here for the floor, but use the packers against the wall to allow for expansion.

Ideally, I think the best way to start is to remove the skirting before you begin laying the new floor. You can lay the floor with the skirting in place, as shown, provided an 8mm (³/₈in) clearance from the skirting is left all around the floor edge.

The new flooring is supplied with a separate foam base on a roll, approximately 6mm (¹/₄in) thick [A], which you simply cut to size and lay on top of the existing floor [B].

Lay the first board against the wall leaving an 8mm (³/₈in) gap between the board and the wall by using pre-cut wooden spacers [C]. Cutting a section to length, simply measure (remember the 5mm gap), mark with a square and cut with either a tenon saw or crosscut saw [D]. Ensure that the saw is sharp. To avoid breakout, score the surface with a craft knife on the line before cutting with the saw. There shouldn't really be any waste because off-cuts can be used. Provided there is a minimum distance of 45.5mm (18in) maintained between joints, that is. Obviously, short off-cuts may not be worth using.

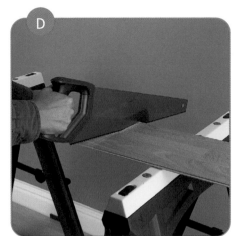

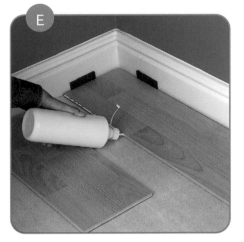

Apply the glue to the end tongue only and complete the first line. Then apply the second line of boards by applying the adhesive along the length as well as the end of the tongue [E]. The flooring is made with a tongue and groove design, which interlocks together for strength, with minimum waste.

Once positioned onto the glued tongue, the board must be tapped home using a claw hammer and a tapping block to tighten up the joints [F]. Wipe away any excess glue that squeezes out straight away with a damp cloth [G].

Continue this process across the room until you have finished the floor. You may have to cut the last board along its length to fit the room (remember to allow for the wooden spacers). When the floor is finished, leave for a minimum of 6 hours to allow the adhesive to cure properly. Then remove the wooden spacers all around. This is very important to allow the floor to expand and contract unrestricted. Finally, cut 20mm (³/₄in)

quadrant to size; apply a thin bead of glue to the skirting face of the quadrant and pin to the skirting ONLY to cover the gap all around, but still allowing the floor to move [H].

And remember; any spills on the floor must be cleaned immediately. To wash the surface, use a tightly squeezed mop – do not use water, otherwise the floor may swell and could be ruined.

Tools Required:

Scissors
Tape measure
Pencil
Hand saw
Set square
Craft knife
Claw hammer
Tapping block
Spacers

FIXING VINYL FLOOR TILES

The first vinyl-type floor tiles I ever laid were for my mum in our kitchen-cum-dining room – that was thirty years ago! I can hear you all saying 'How could he possibly have done that job at the age of five!' Thank you all for that gesture, it was so kind. And I wasn't a day over seven!

Seriously though, I was just fifteen, and these tiles weren't so much vinyl, more linoleum tiles, with a hessian backing. They were also as tough as old boots!

The floorboards were all over the place, so I had to pin down some sheeting to level up the floor. I pinned down some hardboard with small ring nails. It looked very good – tight joints, and nice and flat as well. The tiles were so thick and hard that I couldn't stick them down – I had a serious problem. Mum was out, and the adhesive on the floor would be going off soon, so I needed a quick fix. I put the tiles in mum's new cooker oven. After a while, a strange smell

started to permeate through the ground floor just as Mum was returning, so I quickly opened the oven to grab the tiles but they were so hot that I burnt my hands and dropped them; half in the oven and half out. I was hopping around the kitchen blowing on my hands and Mum was chasing me around trying to whack me over the head for ruining her new cooker. To this day she still can't fathom out why I wanted to grill the tiles...

I have to admit, apart from what you've read here, the tiles were not particularly successful once they were laid in position. Being very brittle, they seemed to damage far too easily. This probably wasn't helped by the fact that I hadn't soaked the hardboard before I laid it, creating a rolling landscape out of the kitchen floor. This was definitely something that Constable might have been proud of – it was a very arresting picture!

Fortunately, vinyl tiles are much easier to use than those I had to deal with all those years ago. In the case of a conventional boarded wooden floor, it is necessary to overlay the floor first either with hardboard or 6mm (¼in) plywood. I prefer the plywood. It is not much more expensive than hardboard, but makes a better job. Fix the plywood or hardboard with 25mm (1in) ring nails.

Vinyl tiles are normally self-adhesive, but store the tiles in the room for a couple of days for them to acclimatize to the room temperature. Mark the centre of two opposite walls and snap a chalk line or string between the two points [A]. Repeat this on the opposite two walls and you'll have a centre point. Lay out some tiles at this point, without

Tools Required:

Hammer
Chalk line
Straight edge
Craft knife
Measuring tape

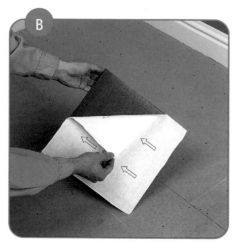

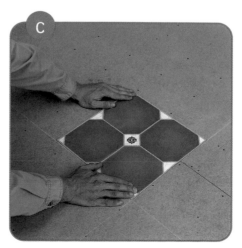

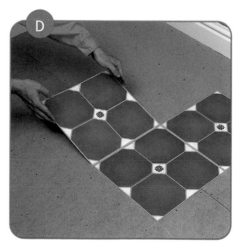

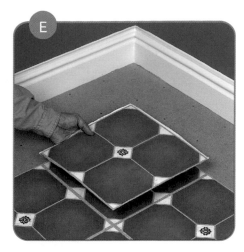

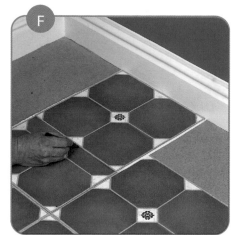

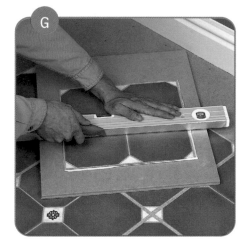

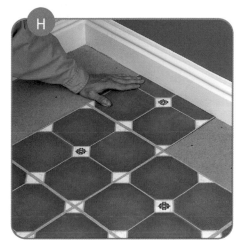

TOMMY'S TIP

Use silicone sealant around the edges of the tiles on bathroom and kitchen floors to give a fully watertight finish. Also, if you have to cut tiles at all, do it on an old piece of board, so that there is no danger of cutting into your beautiful, newly laid floor!

removing the protective backing, to see the most effective way of fixing them with minimum wastage and balanced cut edges.

Mark your starting position. Lift the tiles and give the floor a final vacuum. Peel the backing off the first tile [B] and carefully place to the marks applying smoothing pressure with your hands [C]. Repeat the process, concentrating on one half of the floor and steadily laying a pyramid shape, carefully butting the tiles together [D].

For trimming in the edges, lay a tile against the wall over the last full tile [E] (without removing the backing) and mark the fixed tile [F]. Transfer the marks onto a tile for cutting with a sharp craft knife and straight edge [G]. Peel the back off and stick the cut tile firmly into place. Now all you have to do is stand back and admire your work.

In a kitchen or bathroom, make sure that the floor and the bottoms of the surrounding walls are absolutely dry and clean before you begin laying the tiles.

Fixing Vinyl Floor Tiles

61

FIXING CERAMIC FLOOR TILES

Well-laid ceramic floor tiles can look very attractive, but before deciding whether you want ceramic or quarry tiling for your floor, bear a few things carefully in mind.

Tiled floors are very cold to the touch, which is ideal in a hot climate like Spain or Portugal but in colder climates they may prove a problem. In an ideal situation, a combination of a tiled floor and under-floor heating may be the solution. Also bear in mind that the surface becomes slippery in stockinged feet, and especially when a spillage occurs. In a kitchen area, a tiled floor is very unforgiving when anything breakable is dropped on it, and if this happens a floor tile could break into the bargain.

On a positive note, a ceramic floor can be hard-wearing, easy to clean, stain-resistant, durable and hygienic, and visually very effective.

There are a couple of particularly popular styles of ceramic floor. The first is a very clean-cut reproduction of a Bath & Portland stone floor, consisting of large plain coloured tiles with the corners angled, and small dark inserts to fix in the corners. This is a very effective pattern, particularly when it is covering a large area. Another popular style, in complete contrast to the first, is that achieved with rustic French terracotta floor tiles. These are particularly popular in large kitchens, open plan areas, stylish conservatories and so on.

Original floor tiles of this type are often expensive and difficult to lay due to the very random nature of their size and thickness. Machine-made reproductions are good value, easy to lay, and can give the desired effect.

The first ceramic floor I remember laying was for my mum in the kitchen/dining room after my unsuccessful foray with lino tiles. To make things more difficult, the tiles Mum had chosen involved a fancy interlocking pattern (very continental in a Victorian terrace), and everyone thought they were wonderful at the time! As mentioned earlier, ours was a very busy household with six children and lots of relations and friends. The kitchen/diner was the magnetic heart of the house, because that's where the food and drink was kept!

Anyway, within about eighteen months, the areas in front of the cooker and around Dad's rocking chair had deteriorated. The glazing wore off, and then the colour, leaving areas of red clay showing through. So it was back to the drawing board. Again.

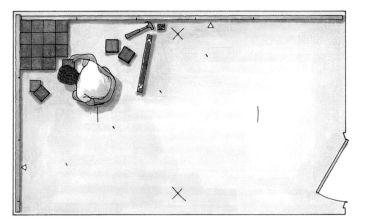

Mark out the floor for tiling with chalk and a tape measure and then set out the field with battens.

Tools Required:

Screwdriver
Measuring tape
Hammer
Pencil
Serrated edge trowel
Rubber float
Sponge
Tile cutter
Straight edge

The ideal surface on which to lay ceramic floor tiles is a level and flat screeded floor. If you have floorboards or a poor, unlevel surface, you may require a sub-floor to be fitted first.

Lay a sub-floor of 12mm ($\frac{1}{2}$in) or 18mm ($\frac{3}{4}$in) plywood, screwed down at centres every 305mm (12in). Apply a sealing coat of PVA adhesive mixed with water over the plywood surface, ready to receive the adhesive.

Mark the centre of all four walls and snap a chalk line on the floor to dissect the floor into quarters. Lay the tiles out dry in one quarter, then mark the floor for fixing two wooden

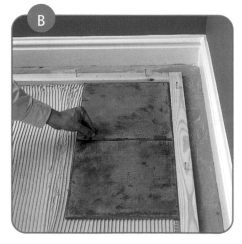

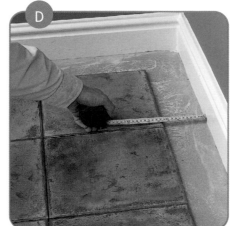

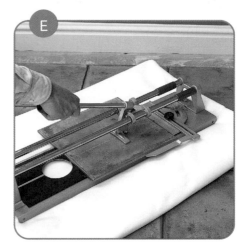

battens. It is very important that the battens are perfectly square. Check this by using the 3:4:5 method. Mark off one batten at 3ft (915mm) and the second batten at 4ft (1220mm); measuring between the two points should equal exactly 5ft (1520mm). The corner should be perfectly square, so secure the battens and apply the adhesive about a square yard (metre) at a time with a serrated trowel [A]. Press the tiles into the adhesive, building out from the corner. Cut a couple of bucketfuls of equal spacers before laying the tiles and fit these between the tiles to form equal size joints [B]. Use a short straight edge (spirit level) to check the tiles are in line [C]. Have a bucket of clean water and a sponge on hand to clean off any excess adhesive. Repeat this process until the whole floor area is covered. Leave for 24 hours to cure, then carefully remove the battens to cut in the edges all round.

Carefully measure both ends of the tile space, and transfer the dimensions to a tile for cutting [D]. Remember to allow for spacers and cut with a mechanical tile cutter [E]. Paste the back of the tile with adhesive and squeeze carefully into place. Check with a level or straight edge that the cuts are laid level with the rest of the tiled floor.

Grout the new tiled floor with a waterproof grout using a rubber float, completing small sections at a time and wiping off the excess with a damp sponge, rinsing regularly [F]. Rub over the joints with a shaped piece of timber or rubber to compress and shape the joints. Once the grouting has cured, give it a final clean and polish with a soft cloth.

Finally, apply a suitable silicone mastic joint between the floor and the walls all around the room, as a seal.

TOMMY'S TIP

Dry-lay a square of tiles in one corner of the room and measure out before spreading the adhesive. This applies to all floor tiles, whether ceramic or vinyl.

REPLACING AND REPAIRING SKIRTING

Skirtings are quite often largely ignored and go generally unnoticed in the greater scheme of things. However, they have an important practical as well as aesthetic role in the function of your home.

In the times of Georgian and Victorian design, skirtings were often very tall; 10 to 12 inches (255–305mm) or more, made in an elaborate design from a compilation of different straight and moulded pieces of softwood. Since Victorian times, the skirtings seem to have shrunk in height and design, as have rooms generally since that time. Modern skirtings have simple uncluttered lines, which often reflect modern design.

The practical function of a skirting, however, has hardly changed at all. It is designed to cover the joint between the wall and floor, concealing the gaps that need to be allowed for expansion and contraction. It's also fitted to protect the decorations, the wallpaper and paint finishes from sweeping brooms (and more recently, vacuum cleaners), the legs of chairs and the feet of young boys as a kicking board. As I have mentioned previously, I am a fan of early period design – particularly Victoriana – and I like tall skirtings, which can be used to conceal all manner of things from central heating pipes to electrical circuits, hi-fi cabling and computer power links.

One thing I would advise though, is to try to keep true to the period of your property. Quite obviously, tall Victorian-style skirtings would look out of place in a modern room with a low ceiling in a 1960s-style property.

REPAIRING DAMAGED SKIRTING

Sometimes it is possible to cut out a piece of skirting and replace it 'in situ', without having to take everything apart. To do this, firstly knock the blade of a small bolster chisel behind the skirting. Lever open a gap to allow the crowbar to fit and place a wooden packer behind the crowbar to protect the wall from damage when levering. Slide a couple of timber blocks down behind the skirting to keep the skirting sprung from the wall [A]. Position the mitre block against the skirting and using the 45º slot, cut the skirting with a tenon saw, using short strokes [B]. Repeat this process to the other side of the damage and remove the offending piece of skirting.

Release the blocks and countersink and screw the skirting back into position into wall plugs. Carefully measure the distance, or use the damaged piece of skirting as a template (remember to allow extra for the saw cuts if you do). Start

Tools Required:

Small bolster chisel
Crowbar
Tenon saw
Mitre block
Coping saw
Pencil
Tape measure
Drill
Countersink
Square
Claw hammer
Pinchers
Nail and pin punch
Mitre saw

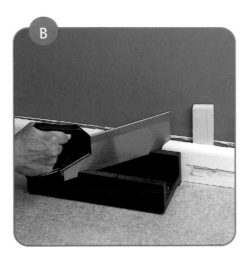

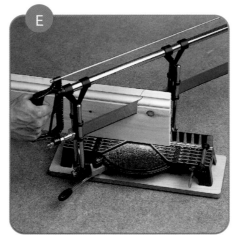

your pins off and add a bead of PVA glue. Hold in position and knock home the pins [C]. Use a pin punch to drive in the pins and a damp cloth to wipe off any excess glue. Use a filler on the pin holes and joints and allow to dry. Sandpaper down, prime, undercoat and top-coat for a successful repair. This is what is know in the trade as 'scarfing'.

REPLACING SKIRTING

Removing the entire skirting involves simply repeating the process mentioned above, moving the levers along and springing the skirting free from the middle [D]. Once the first piece is freed, the rest should spring free in sequence.

A good buy is a mitre saw, which will come in handy for lots of different jobs. If you are the most fortunate person in the country and your internal corner is perfectly square, it may be possible to cut an internal mitre which won't look like a 'pigs ear' [E]! It does take time to master a mitre saw, though. It is sometimes

possible to fix skirting directly into masonry or brickwork with masonry nails, but you may find battens easier [F].

An external mitre should be cut, glued and pinned together, ensuring a perfect square fit and closed joint [G]. For extra strength, fix a couple of pins through the mitre itself [H].

TOMMY'S TIP

When pinning through a mitre, make a pilot hole first by putting a pin into your drill and using it as a drill bit. This will prevent splitting the relatively thin and delicate mitre.

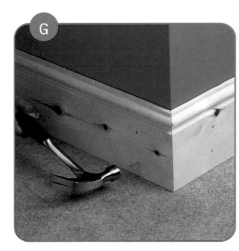

The Victorians were great exponents of beautiful ceilings, whether they were wonderfully ornate or subtly plain. I have just acquired a large Victorian terraced house purely because it is my favourite period, and the ceilings in the living rooms are 12 feet (3.7m) high. All that is left is a 6 foot length (1.8m) of the original cornice – the rest of the ceilings have been plastered over. The one good thing about buying a derelict period property is the challenge and excitement of restoring it to its former glory. (I must be mad!)

The first time I took on a major ceiling restoration job always reminds me of the *Only Fools and Horses* classic episode in which Del Boy is attempting to clean the huge chandelier in a big country mansion. Just as everything appeared to be going well, disaster befell him!

The cornice we were restoring had been painted so many times over the years that all the detail had been covered up. This would take ages to strip. Luckily, there was a new chemical compound available for stripping off built-up

coatings on cornices. We spread the compound over the cornice, covered it with a special cellophane sheet, and left it overnight to cure. In the morning, we peeled off the special sheet, taking a large amount of the build up with it. I was really pleased with the result, so I repeated the process. It was lucky for me that I'd only done one length, because when I peeled off the sheet, not only did it remove the excess material, it also removed part of the cornice!

I knew how Del Boy felt when the wrong chandelier came down in the programme and I just wanted to escape, as he did! Nevertheless, I had to set about repairing the damage.

Fortunately, an old friend of mine, Jimmy Thompson, had a fibrous plaster company and he saved my bacon. By taking a mould from the original, he made two new lengths of cornice in his workshop for me. When I had completed the whole job with the new sections in place, all beautifully decorated, the ceiling looked absolutely wonderful. The client was really delighted! (And none the wiser!)

FITTING COVING

Take an off-cut of your cove or cornice, offer it up and mark the walls and ceilings in every corner [A]. Using a chalk line, pin one end onto a mark and stretch a line tautly to the other mark. Carefully snap the line to leave the chalk marks around the whole room. Scratch the finish plaster within the lines with the edge of a scraper to create a key for the adhesive. Apply a solution of PVA adhesive and water to the prepared surface. This prevents the plaster from sucking the water from the adhesive and helps with adhesion.

MAKING A MITRE BLOCK

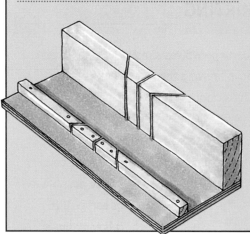

If you fit a lot of coving, it is worth making a mitre block to help you cut accurate joints. Cut a baseboard about 200mm (8in) wide and 450mm (1ft 6in) long. Cut and fix a fence and stop batten as shown, using nails and glue. Cut and mark three sawcuts into the fence, one at rightangles and two at 45°, opposite to each other. These will guide your sawcuts when cutting the coving.

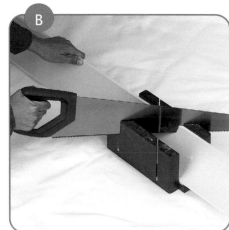

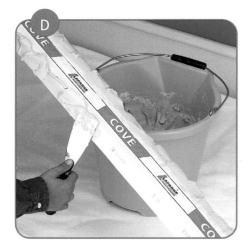

A paper template is usually provided with the coving to enable you to cut the internal and external mitre joints. An easier way to cut a mitre is by using a big mitre block, which you can buy [B] or very easily make. See the box (left). Four different mitres are required – left and right internal, and left and right external.

The fixing adhesive is supplied in bags of dry powder, which you simply add to water and mix. To make mixing quicker and easier, a mixing tool can be purchased from a DIY store to fit into your electric drill. Remember to use the slow speed [C]! The mixture should have the consistency of clotted cream and be applied either with a pointing trowel or filling knife [D].

Don't fret if the mitres are not perfect because the joints can be filled and shaped with some of the excess adhesive. On a cornice however, the joints would have to be over-filled with casting plaster when set, and the pattern cut out with a special

weapon called a 'trowel end small tool'. They come in a range of different shapes and sizes, but are basically like a long steel drawer handle with a spoon shape at one end (for applying plaster) and a blade shape at the other end (for carving).

When pressing coving (or cornice) into position, the crucial guide to follow is the chalk line on the wall, because that's the line that the eye will see [E]. Quite often the ceilings are out of plumb, but you can pack any gaps with adhesive or filler and when painted, it will never notice. So don't try to force the coving or cornice to meet both surfaces, keep it straight and fill any gaps.

Carefully scrape off the excess adhesive with a filling knife or trowel then rub over with a damp sponge to remove all traces of excess adhesive and leave a nice smooth finish [F]. Finally, I find that some nails temporarily hammered in underneath the cove or cornice very useful, as it will hold the coving or cornice in place whilst the adhesive goes off [G].

TOMMY'S TIP

For coving, you really do need a mitre block – a set-square simply isn't up to the job...

Tools Required:

Mitre block
Saw
Pointing trowel
Scraper
String line
Tape measure
Hammer
Screwdriver

FITTING DADO AND PICTURE RAILS

Isn't it strange what is sometimes in fashion and what's not? Hairstyles come to mind – they're always a poignant reminder of a particular period, with footballers being a great example! Just look back at the Seventies and Eighties. Remember the long layered hair with extended sideburns, or the Kevin Keegan perm! When those footballers look back at their early pictures it must bring a smile (or a cringe) to their faces. Having said that, I can't really talk – I once allowed my wife to perm my hair and I had blonde highlights to boot! I remember looking in the mirror and thinking 'you stupid plonker, you look as though an old crow's nest has just landed on your head!'

Needless to say, that particular hairstyle didn't last very long, but fashions do change constantly. In fact, I'm waiting for the 'Lionel Blair's' (flairs) that I wore with that haircut to come back into style... I kept a couple of pairs to keep 'ahead of the game' and so that my kids might think I'm a 'cool dude'!

Dado and picture rails are sort of 'victims of fashion', as well! They have a very practical use though, which was the original design concept. The picture rail was designed for just that – a decorative feature fixed around a room to hang pictures on. No need to drill holes in your walls or any danger of banging nails through pipes or cables! The picture rail also created a break line, allowing for more creative decorating in the room as a whole.

The same can be said for the dado rail. Classic decoration can be achieved by fixing two dado rails: the first a large detailed rail, and the second, a lower rail – smaller and finer in detail – with a decorative paper border fitted between the two. The dado's practical function was to protect the walls and decorations from the backs of chairs set out along the walls. There may not be a need for such caution today, but the original dado and picture rail features are very much the trend in particular types of homes.

So the Sixties, Seventies and Eighties may have witnessed the ripping out of these features, but the new millennium is seeing a reversal in their fortunes which is putting them back in vogue! However, if you ever expect to see me wearing that crow's nest hairstyle, forget it! 'Permed and blonde' – I just hope nobody still has a photograph!

Tools Required:

Measuring tape
Mitre block
Mitre saw
Nail punch
Spirit level
Hammer
Cordless drill
Tenon saw
Filling knife
Sealant gun

Mark the desired position of the dado rail on the walls. The height you select to fix the rail at is your choice, but it may look odd if it is much higher than a metre (3ft 3in) from the floor. Using a spirit level, rotating it as you go, draw a line around the room [A]. The height of a picture rail is usually about 300–500mm (1ft– 1ft 8in) below the ceiling cornice. To cut a dado or picture rail to length, you will need a mitre block and tenon saw, or a mitre saw [B]. When joining two pieces at a corner, mitre the ends to make a perfect 90° angle.

You can now buy special adhesives to fix timber features such as picture and dado rails. Just apply the adhesive with a

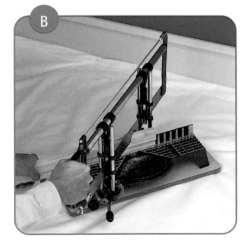

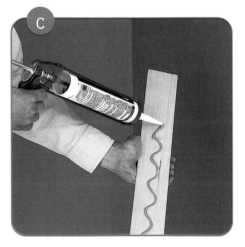

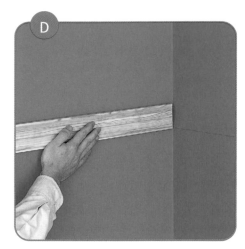

sealant gun [C], and press the rail into place [D]. In the case of a modern wall constructed from timber studwork (framework) and plasterboard, use 50–65mm (2–2¹/₂in) lost head nails through the rail fixed into the vertical studwork timbers. Knock the nails below the surface using a punch [E]. Fill the nail holes afterwards with proprietary filler.

If you are lucky, then the corners of your room might be nice and square. That would enable you to cut an internal mitre to fit the corners perfectly. Another way to cut two pieces for an internal corner, is to cut one piece square ended and fix it, then to scribe the second piece over the first. A scribe is obtained by first cutting an internal mitre. Using a coping saw, cut off the mitre leaving just the profile. This should then fit snugly over the first piece [F].

Two pieces of rail can be joined together by means of mitring on a 45° angle and fixing the first piece. Mitre the second piece to fit perfectly over the first, using a touch of PVA [G]. Add an extra bit of strength to an external corner by knocking in a pin or two [H].

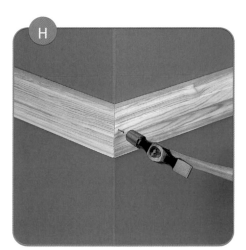

TOMMY'S TIP

It's much easier to sandpaper the rails before they go on the wall. Remember, 'the finish is only as good as the preparation!'

FITTING A FIREPLACE SURROUND

We've all seen it on film and television – the perfect setting. It's a winter's night, so it's cold and dark outside. The camera pans. Inside, the lighting is subtle; the furniture and decor consist of warm, sensual colours. There's a huge rug on the floor between the armchairs and sofa where a couple look adoringly at each other, each sipping a large Bailey's over ice. The ice is in stark contrast to the beautiful roaring fire just a few feet in front of them. Sounds great doesn't it?

Our fascination with fire is not so strange. It offers us warmth and security which goes all the way back to our creation! 'That's all very well', I hear you say 'but how do I fit one in my living room? Where do I start?'

I've always thought that the focal point of any family or living room is the fireplace. With the advent of central heating and changes in building design, the fireplace has become a major casualty, with thousands of people boarding them up, and worse still, completely removing the chimney breasts (the brick and plaster projections which house the flue to remove smoke and dangerous gases from the room). Inevitably, the outcome of these trends causes a bit of a vacuum and people look back lovingly, trying to recreate the ambience of a real fire. Hence we have come full circle, and as with many fashions, they are back in vogue, and it's not necessarily difficult to reproduce the effect.

If you don't have a chimney breast in your room, do not despair – the surround can fit straight onto the wall. (An outside wall though, if you want to fit a gas fire.) You could build a dummy breast for effect, and fit the fire surround to that! If you're lucky enough to have a chimney breast in the room, then that's the place to fix the fire surround. Ensure the chimney is checked and swept by a qualified chimney sweep if you intend to use it as a proper fireplace, with either an open coal or gas fire.

The surround featured in the photographs is purely decorative and can be fixed to a straight wall or chimney breast. This surround is purchased as a kit, with a pine surround and imitation marble insert and hearth.

First put a centre mark on the wall and hearth so they align [A]. Turn the hearth on to its face (make sure the face is protected with a dustsheet) then apply adhesive or silicone mastic to the hearth framework [B] and fix into position, using the alignment marks [C]. Then check its level.

Place the mantel assembly upside down; slide the legs into position, then screw the block inside the mantel assembly [D]. To secure the legs, first check they are square to the mantel and then screw them in place with 6 x 35mm (1³⁄₈in) screws. For a simple method of fixing this surround to the wall, screw two mirror plates with screws to the back edge of

TOMMY'S TIP

Make sure the hearth is fitted with the help of a plumb line or spirit level, otherwise the fireplace may look off balance with the room. Also, if you wish to have a painted or varnished finish, ensure you carefully sandpaper down the pine surround while it is on the floor for a good finish.

Tools Required:

Tape measure
Spirit level
Screwdriver
Drill
Pilot bit
Mastic gun

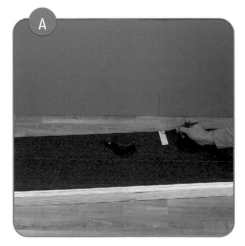

the legs approximately 230mm (9in) from the top [E]. Next fix the marble effect insert to the surround as shown, with screws approximately 380mm (15in) apart [F]. Remember to pre-drill pilot holes for the screws to avoid break-out damage.

Offer up the surround and mark the hole positions on the wall through the mirror plates [G]. Remove the surround, drill and plug the wall, and then fix the surround with screws.

The final act is to place the reveal insert into position, to cover the wall behind and leave a clean neat finish [H].

WORKING FIREPLACES

There is nothing to beat a working fireplace on a cold winter's night, or over Christmas! Talk to the suppliers before you purchase the surround you require, to ensure it is safe to use with the working fire you have, or intend to use.

Very importantly; all gas fires MUST be installed by a CORGI-registered gas installer, who will ensure safe installation of an appliance in your home. Insist on checking his CORGI certificate papers, and make sure the papers are up-to-date.

STRIPPING WALLS AND CEILINGS

Stripping walls and ceilings can only be described as very hard work. I should know – I've done enough of it over the years! In certain circumstances there is a case for leaving on the old paper, but a really good job requires stripping off (the old paper I mean!), and preparing the walls and ceilings properly.

As my Dad would always tell me, 'If a job's worth doing, it's worth doing properly!' This is achieved by purchasing a really good decorating kit. The scrapers, brushes, and so on should be of good quality, and always allow yourself time at

the end of the job to clean your tools properly. Contrary to popular opinion, paintbrushes work much better as they wear down through use. Like any tool, they need to be broken in to give the best finish. Using new brushes every time you paint is not good practice, and it's an expensive habit, as good quality brushes are not cheap! However, before using a new brush, I usually wash it out, which helps to remove loose bristles and any dust. A good decorating set should last the average DIY-er a lifetime, providing you don't let anyone else get their hands on it!

STRIPPING WALLPAPER

Before you actually begin stripping your walls, remove the carpets and underlay, roll them up, tie them with string and store them away. Score the walls all over with the edge of your scraper or a wallpaper scorer [A], and soak the paper with warm soapy water and a sponge. The next important thing you need is patience. To make this task easier, remember that the more you soak the paper, the easier it will be to strip off. Work a rotation system on the walls – in between stripping one, keep soaking the other.

Ceilings are a lot more difficult to strip, depending on what paint has been used over the paper. I would suggest that you either buy or hire a steam stripper as they're useful for walls also [B]. They are also now very reasonably priced and are always handy for future redecoration.

When using a steam stripper, follow the instructions carefully and adhere to the safety advice. Don't hold the steamer in one place for too long or you may loosen the plaster finish coat on old walls. Well-soaked wallpaper should practically fall off. A lot of plaster damage can occur by using the scraper forcefully on paper that has not been soaked through thoroughly [C]. If in doubt, peel the paper off by hand.

TOMMY'S TIP

When you're going to strip walls, expect to be patient and to create mess. Protect the floor surface from water drips and falling paper, and have a sponge to hand for the really stubborn bits.

Tools Required:

Steps
Trestles
Steam stripper
Club hammer
Bolster chisel
Scrapers
Wallpaper scorer
Wire brush
Gloves and goggles
Sponge
Paddle brush

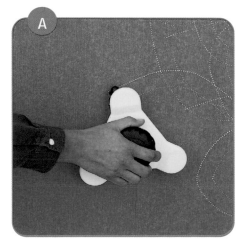

When stripping wallpaper directly above a socket or light switch, turn off the power supply temporarily, and loosen off the socket and switch faces, to allow for the paper to be completely removed. Make sure sockets are dry before switching the power back on.

Some wallpapers allow you to strip off the face of the paper leaving just the backing paper as the lining. If it is sound, the backing paper can be left on, and this can save a lot of time and energy.

To remove the backing paper, soak with warm, slightly soapy water applied with a paddle brush [D]. Apply at least two soakings allowing approximately 20 minutes to soak through. When all the paper is removed from the walls with a scraper [E], and all the waste is cleared from the floor and

disposed of in plastic bags, wash the walls down with a warm water and mild detergent solution.

REMOVING CERAMIC TILES

One of the most important things to remember when removing tiles from the wall is safety. Goggles and gloves are essential, as sharp splinters can be created when removing tiles, and broken edges can be as sharp as a razor. Break out one tile first [F]. This will allow you to get the bolster chisel behind the next tile more easily. Use the bolster and hammer to remove the old adhesive as you go. Clean the walls and clear the floor as you go also.

Very old, pre-Edwardian wall tiling was generally fixed with a sharp sand and cement mix. This is extremely tough to remove and will require re-plastering of the walls where the removal of any tiles has taken place.

STRIPPING CEILINGS

This is not an easy task and it is essential to use a steam stripper. Most importantly, set up a safe platform to work from, NOT a mere stepladder! Use trestles and a youngman's platform and spend time setting this up at a comfortable height. You will only be able to work for short spells at a time. Working overhead, your arms will feel like lead, so work at a steady pace across the ceiling and take frequent breaks.

PREPARING WALLS AND CEILINGS FOR DECORATION

I look back on some of the jobs that I have had to do over the years and wonder how we ever managed to get such a marvellous finish, considering what we started with. In fact, it's a classic case of actually making a 'silk purse out of a sow's ear'! For the record, and the sake of political correctness, I do not intend any pain to pigs, neither mental nor physical. And by way of reinforcing that statement, I would like to add that I like pigs a hell of a lot! Boiled bacon and cabbage is my favourite meal!

My Dad would always say, 'The finished job is only as good as the preparation gone into it.' Most professionals would agree with that, so always bear that wise little statement firmly in mind whenever you are doing your own work at home or whenever you are tempted to slack!

There was a guy called Ian we used to sub-contract for on the building side, who was a highly regarded decorator – we used to watch in bewilderment at how much filler he used on a house. His policy was to strip the walls of paper, spread filler over all the walls and then sand it off. I was amazed because it appeared to be such a waste of materials and labour, although at the end there was a good finish to the decorating. I'm not suggesting that anyone should do what he does, but remember that the decorated finish is what everyone is going to see – particularly you!

If you have rushed the preparation work prior to decorating, every time you walk in the room, the bits that you are not happy with will stand out so much to you that it will drive you crazy. So, please take your time and prepare properly! Even the roughest of walls can be immensely improved.

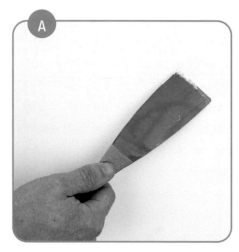

In your extensive good quality decorating kit, there should be at least a couple of filling knives, both broad and narrow bladed. These look exactly the same as scrapers, but are much more flexible, enabling the filling process to be carried out much more effectively than if you used a scraper.

Often in older properties, when the paper is removed, areas of finish plaster (the top coat) come away from the base coat. Ensure that the topcoat edges are stable, but do not insert your scraper under the finish or you will pop off more and more of the surface. In preparation of plaster damage, always cut and scrape towards the centre from the sides. As I said, prepare your whole wall, and apply a solution of PVA adhesive and water to the dry damaged areas with a paintbrush. 'Knock-up' your filler by adding water to the powder, and apply it to the damaged sections. To areas where there is a crack, cut out the crack to form a 'V' shape using the corner of the scraper. Apply the PVA and water solution, and fill [A]. When sanding down, you'll probably only need fine grade paper. Fold the paper and rub lightly over the filled surface until smooth [B].

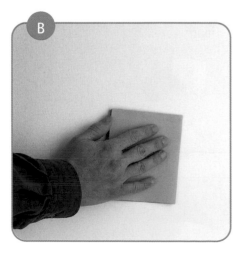

Tools Required:

Scrapers
Filler knifes
Sponge
Mastic gun
Mastic
Hammer
Batten
Sandpaper
Craft knife

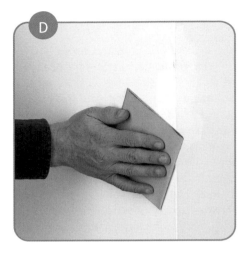

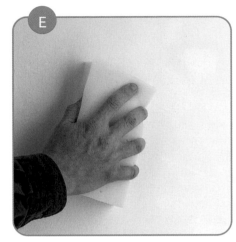

Quite often corners get damaged, as they are far more vulnerable to getting knocked. Pinning a temporary batten to the wall and filling in the gaps will easily rectify this [C].

Leave it overnight to cure, then remove the batten and fill in the pinholes. When dry, sand the surface [D].

When the room is sanded down and the dust swept up or vacuumed, use clean water and a sponge to rinse over the walls to remove any residue or debris before redecorating [E].

There are lots of new decorating aids available on the market today. One of these, decorator's caulk, is very handy. This is mastic in a tube, which you apply with a mastic gun. When you purchase mastic, ensure that you buy the correct one for the job. There is a wide range available to do a variety of jobs. For decorating, you need a water-soluble decorator's caulk (NOT silicone). This caulk is wonderful for flexible filling between the walls and skirtings or around door and window architraves. You may find you have different size cracks to fill, so start by cutting off just the tip of the caulk nozzle applicator with a craft knife and fill all the narrow cracks [F]. For broader cracks cut off more of the nozzle to create a wider bead.

Using these mastic guns effectively takes a bit of practice. I recommend that you start at the top and in a smooth flowing motion, apply the bead in a steady line along the crack. Remember to release the trigger to cut off the mastic flow at the end of the run, or it will ooze out everywhere!

Smooth off the caulk with a damp sponge, regularly rinsing out the sponge to avoid any mess. We used to use our fingers years ago – lick it first, then rub along the joint. Let me tell you, it doesn't taste very nice and you end up absolutely covered in the stuff, so I wouldn't recommend this method!

TOMMY'S TIP

Prepare and fill at least one wall at a time and leave overnight to cure before rubbing down. Also, seal the wall with PVA adhesive solvent.

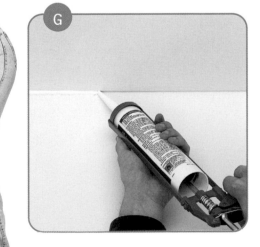

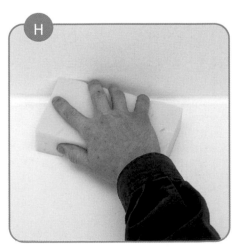

PAINTING WALLS AND CEILINGS

This is the interesting part of the job – all the laborious stripping and preparation has been done. This is where the transformation takes place – the pleasurable bit where you reap the benefits of all your hard prep work!

I've always been a fan of painted walls and ceilings – I think because the effect is so instant. I'm going back to the first time when I was given my own room – it wasn't particularly big, but it was mine, and it was right next to the bathroom, which was tough on my sisters. I must have been about 14 years of age at the time (you know, that obnoxious age), and I had to pay for the redecoration from my Saturday and holiday jobs. Heavy rock was popular at the time – Led Zeppelin, Black Sabbath – I mention this because this influenced the colour scheme I chose, which

was bright orange and black. Yes, orange and black! My design was contrasting – two opposite walls were orange and the other two were black. The skirtings were orange on the black wall, and black on the orange, and the ceiling was a chessboard of painted orange and black polystyrene tiles. And of course, it was finished off with a magnificent orange carpet! How in heaven's name could anyone sleep in that room? But I did, and I thought I was really cool! I remember my dad looked in, then left mumbling and shaking his head. But I have to say, the finish quality was good because of the preparation work. The colour schemes I choose now, though, seem very tame by comparison. I wonder what my wife would say if I was to suggest a colour scheme along similar lines?

When painting ceilings the best method is to use a lambswool roller [A]. If possible, fit an extension pole to enable you to reach the ceiling comfortably from the floor, but if this isn't possible, set up a safe, sturdy work platform. Please remember to cover the floor with dustsheets and use the roller slowly across the ceiling, or you'll soon have more paint on the floor than you have on the ceiling. The roller will only take the paint close to the walls. The edges of the ceiling will have to be painted using a brush [B]. This brushwork is known as 'cutting in'. If this overlaps onto the walls a bit, it doesn't matter, as the wall colour will cover that overlap when it is applied. If you have a coving or a cornice, this should be incorporated into the ceiling colour – unless you wish to make it stand out in its own colour.

When painting walls, again the best method is to use a roller – not too vigorously, or the paint will splash onto the

woodwork and the newly painted ceiling. Using the roller, cover the walls with the paint [C]. The bits the roller can't reach will have to be completed with a brush. Splashes on the woodwork or walls should be removed while still wet with a damp sponge or cloth.

Using a brush and cutting in at ceiling level requires a steady hand [D] and a confident heart, so make sure you stick to drinking only tea, at least until the room's finished.

Talking of tea, or if you have to pop out or do something in between coats, you can wrap the roller and brushes in cling film to prevent them from going crusty before you've finished using them [E]. Mind you don't slip up and pop them into the fridge though!

There's always that awkward space behind the radiator that needs doing. If you don't want the aggro of taking off the rad, then simply use a rad roller to reach as far down or up as you will need to go [F].

Tools Required:

Dust sheets
Roller
Roller tray
Brushes
Stepladder
Platform
Radiator roller
Cling film (but not
for your sandwiches)

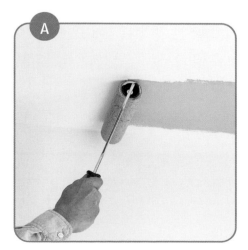

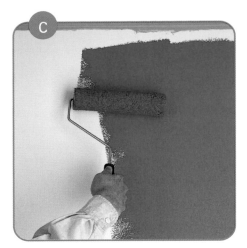

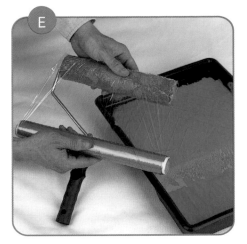

From the health and safety point of view, it's very important that any ladders or platforms are safely constructed and positioned. Stairwells are a common problem, but tailor-made platforms for these areas are available to hire or you can build your own.

When you need to decorate your stairwell, you can build your own tailor-made platform with an interlocking network of scaffold boards, stepladders and boxes. Ensure that you bind cloth around the heads of ladders to protect the walls they lean up against, lash all scaffold boards firmly to their supports and screw horizontal surfaces down whenever possible. Remember, safety is the key!

TOMMY'S TIP

When you've finished with the paint and want to store the remainder, push the lid on tightly then spin the paint upside down for a few seconds and turn it back upright. This process allows for an air-tight seal to form around the lid, so that when you re-use the tin, there won't be a thick skin on top of the paint.

HANGING WALLPAPER

My first experience with wallpaper happened around the age of eight years old. I was told by my teacher to cover my books! I'm from a large family, so there wasn't any money available for luxuries like book covers, so I had to make do with covering my books with some old wallpaper leftovers. I wouldn't have minded (in fact, I thought the whole exercise was a waste of time), but the only wallpaper left in our house was the off-cuts from Gran's bedroom – with a pattern of nice large, pink roses!

Everyone knows how mercilessly honest kids are, and they just voiced the truth – the books did look pretty stupid. My mum said, 'take no notice' as mums do, but for me it became a question of honour, and I would learn the art of boxing in defence of Granny's roses on a daily basis.

That was a thorny enough issue to deal with and I'm sure I remain scarred to this day, because I have never used flowered wallpaper since! In fact, the first wallpaper hanging I ever did was when I acquired my own bedroom (known affectionately as my 'orange and black' period!). I was only 14 years old, and after stripping the walls and ceiling, Dad told me to line the walls with lining paper. The house was built in 1860, but a new rear addition was added in 1939, which was where my bedroom was located. The walls were perfectly plastered and didn't need lining paper at all. Two, no three, lessons he taught me on that occasion – how to hang wallpaper, the value of money (mine), and don't trust your father whenever he has a twinkle in his eyes and a wry smile on his lips!

I am right handed, so I like to start to the left of the door and work my way around the room – from right to left. An alternative method is to start between two windows, or the centre of a chimneybreast, particularly if the paper has a large and impressive pattern. Then you should ensure that, upon entering the room, the prominent focal point your eyes find is the position that you set the paper out from.

Once you've decided on your starting position, the first thing to do is to mark a vertical level line on the wall using either a plumb line and bob, or a long spirit level, rotating the level as you mark.

Offer the end of the wallpaper to the ceiling [A]. Allow surplus paper for trimming, both top and bottom. Pre-cut enough lengths to cover at least one wall. Check to make sure you have allowed enough paper to enable a match on well spaced repeating patterns. These lengths of paper are known as 'drops'.

Roll out all the drops that you have pre-cut face down on a pasting table ready for pasting. Cover the whole table surface (so no paste gets onto the face of the paper). Apply the paste using a large pasting brush, pasting away from the centre. Fold the pasted paper in a concertina shape paste-to-paste, and face-to-face. Set aside the drops to soak and apply a coat of watery paste to the walls. This is

Tools Required:

Pasting bench
Paste brush
Craft knife
Seam roller
Paper shears
Paper brush
Sponge
Oilstone
Plumb bob
Spirit level

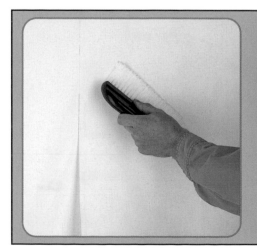

LINING WALLS

When I am decorating, I prefer to double-line a poor wall before hanging paper, if I have the time. This basically involves first covering the wall in lining paper vertically and then going over it a second time horizontally. Obviously this doubles the work involved, but the finished results make the extra effort worthwhile.

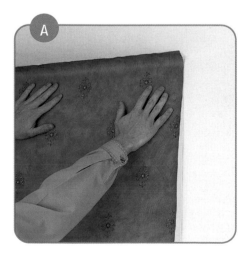

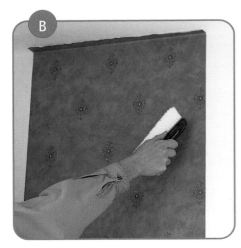

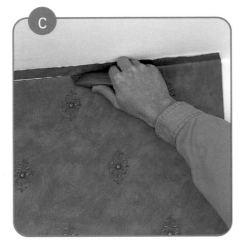

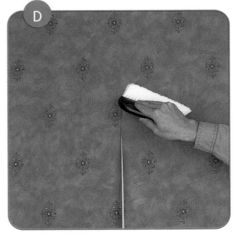

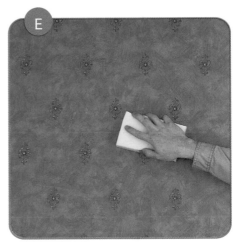

called sizing, and will make hanging the paper much easier, and also prevent the plaster soaking up the paste from the paper.

Offer the first pasted drop up to the ceiling and manoeuvre the drop parallel to the marked line, allowing for trimming. Carefully brush from the centre of the paper out towards the edges moving any trapped air bubbles [B]. Continue this procedure to the whole length of the drop. Using a thin straight edge, tuck

TOMMY'S TIP

Always check that the paper is the right way up as you hang it. On vague patterns such as this one, you will see that the design differs slightly on the left to the right. As you hang each piece, make sure you repeat this pattern.

the paper right into the ceiling joint and trim with a very sharp craft knife [C]. Repeat this process at skirting level.

Take the next drop and repeat the process, ensuring that the pattern matches and the edges butt, as you brush out any air bubbles [D]. Use a damp sponge to sponge off any excess paste to the paper, ceiling and woodwork surfaces as you go [E]!

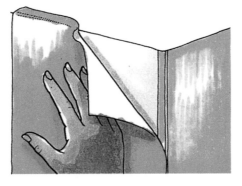

To paper around an internal corner, cut a piece so that it covers the overlap on the first wall. If the piece you trimmed off at the corner is wide enough, use it as your first length on the new wall.

To paper around an external corner, trim the last length so that it wraps around the corner, overlapping by about 25mm (1in). Hang the last strip with its edge about 12mm (½in) from the corner.

FIXING WALL TILES

The first time I ever fixed wall tiles, I made the mistake that comes naturally with youthful arrogance. I couldn't be bothered to fix a batten to the wall because I would be so quick – I would be finished and off to the pub early. I just marked the wall with a level, applied the adhesive and started fixing the tiles.

That would have been fine with a lot of experience and some of the adhesives that are available today, but this was, well, a good few years ago, and yes, before you ask, it was after the advent of horsehair and cow poo plaster...! The tiles all started to move – they were so thick and heavy. Also, I wouldn't pay for spacers – which was a BIG MISTAKE! It was a classic case of more haste less speed. As I did start half-cocked, the problems went from bad to worse, and after a good few hours battling with it, I had to make the embarrassing decision to strip all the work off, clean the tiles and walls which took another long time, and start again, using a batten and setting out properly. I made a 'proper job' of it in the end. But as for going out early with my friends, this became a 'night out on the tiles' with a different meaning! It taught me to spend an extra hour setting out and planning at the beginning, rather than four hours at the end trying to correct faults, which become compounded as you carry on. I still didn't buy the spacers though, so I had to use something else! Read on.

Firstly, take a length of batten approximately 1900mm (6ft 3in) long. Carefully lay out some of your tiles with spacers, marking the batten to create a gauging rod. Offer the rod up to the wall to determine where to start and to keep the cuts at the top, bottom and both corners as equal as possible.

Once the position is established, fix a full horizontal batten above the skirting at that point, using a spirit level. Also fix a vertical batten near the corner. Drill and fix these battens with screws and plugs [A]. With these in place you now have the guides to proceed.

Using a serrated trowel or spreader, apply the adhesive evenly over the wall, covering no more than approximately a square metre at a time [B]. Wall tile adhesive usually comes pre-mixed in large tubs. Press the tiles firmly into the adhesive, remembering to insert the spacers. Once all the full tiles are fixed, remove the battens [C] ready to prepare and place 'the cuts' all around the edges.

Tools Required:

- Tile nibblers
- Gauge stick
- Spirit level
- Pencil
- Drill
- Screws and plugs
- Serrated spreader
- Rubber spreader
- Tile cutter
- Felt-tip pen
- Clean cloth
- Sponge

TOMMY'S TIP

I've often used broken down lengths of thick spaghetti as tile spacers; if you get peckish you can always crunch on a bit of the pasta to keep away hunger pangs! Of course, if you do this, it's much, much easier if the spaghetti is uncooked!

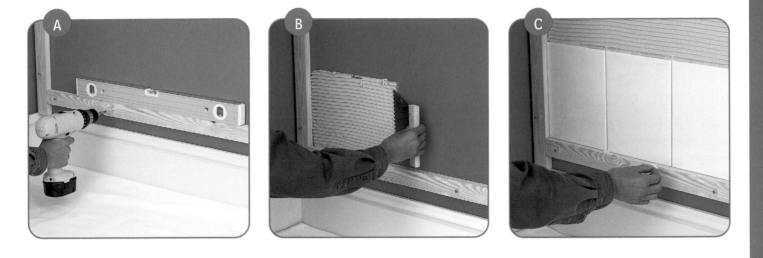

Cutting the tiles is best and fairly effortlessly carried out using a hand operated tile cutter. To mark a tile for cutting, hold it face down into the corner and mark with a felt tip pen, allowing for spacers. Cut the tile [D]. Spread the adhesive on the back of the cut tile and place it carefully in position.

The grouting material is purchased in powder form, which must be made into a creamy paste by adding water. The best method of application is to use a rubber-grouting float (a wooden handled float with a rubber face), which allows you to push the grout around into all the joints easily [E].

It is important to remove all the excess grout from the surface before it goes off. The most effective method is to use a bucket of clean water and a damp sponge. To finish off, polish the tiles with a dry cloth.

To add a little finesse to the job, rub the lines between the tiles over with a jointer to compress and finish the joints [F].

Shape a piece of wood or plastic to make a perfectly good tool. Finally, polish the tiles once more with a dry cloth to finish the job with style.

TILE TOOLS

A tile saw is a very handy tool for cutting shapes out of ceramic tiles – useful for tiling around pipes and so on. Tile nibblers are also very handy for cutting shapes.

Tile Saw   Tile nibblers

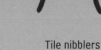

CREATING A DECORATIVE WALL PANEL EFFECT

On the odd occasion in my life things have, thankfully, gone according to plan – like the time I designed a simple project, costing only a few pounds, that transformed a large, fairly plain lounge into a magnificent-looking room. Achieving this gave me a sense of warm self-satisfaction (smugness really, I suppose) – a feeling of 'that was really clever' and 'wow, nothing has gone wrong!' It all seemed so simple, in fact, that it was as if anyone could feel confident about tackling this particular task – even my television director J.T., who has the irritating habit of interrupting in times of intense concentration, especially during a really difficult piece of intricate work, with the words: 'If it were me!' At this point, if J.T. was allowed to continue, he would deliver a complete DIY monologue of how 'I did it in my house!'

Frankly, I'm not even mildly interested in how he does it himself indoors!

This occasional, predictable interjection by J.T. never ceases to raise the hackles on my neck, the result of which is normally observed by the crew, who make bets on whether I'm fast enough to catch him and find a parking spot for that heavy yard broom I'm waving! I have to admit that J.T. has many talents, not least one for finding not my 'G' spot but my 'F' spot (frustration). If you read this John, this is a project just for you – and don't make a 'ficknockle' out of it. ('Ficknockle' being a Norfolk description of a rustic appearance – aka a 'cock up'!)

The room I'm portraying here is plain with only a dado rail to provide any relief to its blandness, so to introduce a bit of interest, I'm going to create a 'decorative wall panel effect'.

Using a tape measure and level, divide the wall into equal panels [A], marking each one off on the wall with a pencil [B]. Stand back and make sure the panel spacing is equal before you proceed any further.

To make an absolutely perfect job of the panelling, draw the wall and panels to scale on a piece of graph paper before you start. This will create the right balance between the positions of the panels before you transfer the dimensions onto the walls.

A mitre saw provides a quick and effective way of cutting the various sections of softwood dado rail needed to make the panelling [C]. Alternatively, use a mitre box and tenon saw to create the same sections.

After sandpapering the cut wood to the desired smoothness, apply knotting fluid with a brush to any knots in the wood. This process effectively prevents the knots from shrinking and

falling out when the heating is turned on and the wood dries out. Paint bare wood with a wood primer [D] before applying undercoat and topcoats of the desired colour. Make sure that you allow the paint to dry completely between coats.

As a rule, I always use two coats of undercoat before applying the topcoat finish. Use very fine sandpaper, known as flour paper, in between coats, to remove any dust and debris and create the perfect finish.

To fix the timber sections to the wall simply and effectively, apply 'Liquid Nails' or 'No Nails' adhesive to the back of the cut lengths [E] and squeeze them carefully into place on the wall [F]. Join the lengths to each other to complete the panel by using PVA whitewood glue on the cut mitre ends.

If you have taken your time and done the job with care, the mitres should fit together perfectly. If this is not the case, do not despair, knock up a bit of the trusty ol' wood filler, and

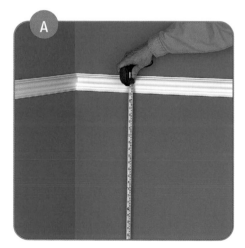

A

B

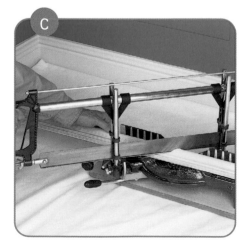

C

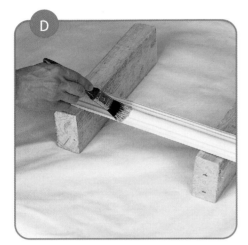

apply it to the mitres with the tip of your finger [G]! Wipe off any excess filler with a damp sponge. Alternatively, you could squeeze a bit of decorator's caulk into the mitre joints, again wiping off the excess with a damp sponge. I actually find this method to be the most effective.

Tools Required:

Tape measure
Spirit level
Mitre saw or
mitre block and
tenon saw
Adhesive
Wood glue
Sponge
Sandpaper
Paint brush

Repeat the process described on all the walls you want to create the effect upon. Allow the adhesive to dry fully and then give it a light rub down with the flour paper. Apply a final finish coat of paint [H]. Stand back and have a good look – you'll be impressed! Inside the panel, the world's your oyster. To contrast with the surrounding wall colour, you could choose a simple painted colour change, maybe a piece of patterned wallpaper, or even a series of landscapes across the panels that would make your local Constable blush!

Tongue and groove panelling is excellent for covering a badly plastered wall or old Victorian tiles that are very difficult to remove. There are some nice designs available on the market today – my favourite is the bead and butt design, which is archetypally Victorian! Also widely available are complete sections of panelling which are simply made up of MDF sheets that are routed out to imitate the Real McCoy. All right, they are fake, but once they are painted, who would know the difference?

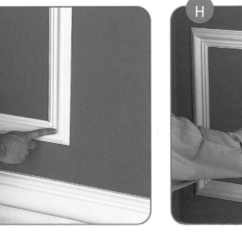

PUTTING UP SHELVES

Shelves. Such a palaver is created about shelves! What type should we have? How should they look? Are they strong enough? How much do they cost? All these questions can be addressed easily enough of course, but in the end the answer is very much down to the individual and how they want the shelves to look. Another important consideration from the construction point of view is what is going to be stacked on the shelves? As a rule of thumb, the wider the shelving, the heavier the gauged thickness of the shelves, with a greater number of supports or fixing points.

To simplify matters, there are basically two main types of shelving – one is the pre-made shelving system, such as 'spur shelving' and the other is 'shelving naturelle', which could be made of anything from glass to granite, or even stainless steel. But I'll show you the simplest and most efficient type of timber shelving for a multitude of uses.

Back in the days before music CDs, the best position for a stereo system was not in a cabinet standing on the floor, but mounted on shelves fixed to the walls. This meant you could dance all night, without the needle jumping and scratching the records. Of course, everybody still needs shelving today, because we still have to store the same things – even though many of them have become miniaturized. A friend of mine 'Smithy' is a music fanatic who used to have thousands of records, which he has now replaced with thousands of CDs. To present these nicely, he commissioned glass shelving over a whole wall. However, although CDs are small and light, collectively they can be enormously heavy, so he still had to reinforce the shelves.

Try to work out roughly what sort of weight you may be loading onto the shelves and construct them accordingly.

The spur shelving system shown on this page is a pre-finished adjustable shelf system, made from mild steel, consisting of vertical wall mounted sections with angled support sections, which simply hook into the wall mounted uprights to create a strong and efficient shelving system.

To fix the spur type of shelving, you first need to fix the vertical supports level and parallel. To achieve this, fix at the top, without tightening the screw right home, plumb it straight with a spirit level, mark and fix the bottom screw. Check that the upright is level when it's against the wall and use packing pieces for adjustment if necessary. Screw home all the fixing points on the upright.

Using the spirit level, match the top of the second upright to the first [A] and repeat the fixing process [B].

The next thing to do is to hook in the shelf supports at the desired heights, then simply cut the shelves to length and attach them to the support brackets via the fixing positions on the undersides of the brackets [C].

The other system of shelving shown here is simply a made-up shelf system which is fixed to the wall, with the fixing

Tools Required:

Spirit level
Drill
Masonry bit
Hammer
Screwdriver
Saw
Tape measure
Sandpaper

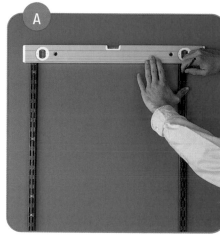

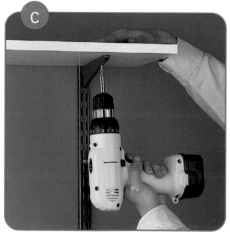

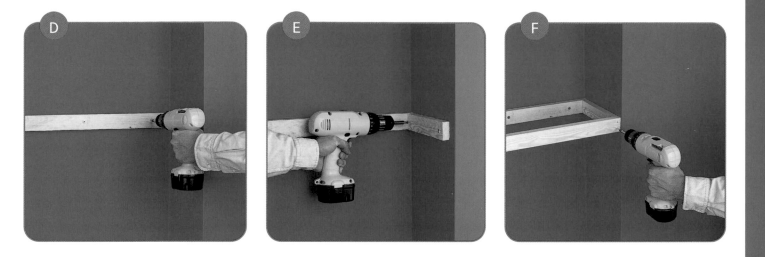

positions concealed from the eye. This is known simply as a 'ladder frame' system and is my preferred type of shelving.

Fixed shelving can be easily installed by using the ladder frame system. Mark the shelf positions with a spirit level on all three sides of the alcove, cut a batten to length and fix with screws and plugs [D]. Next, fix the two side battens in the same way [E]. Cut the fourth batten to length and fix with two screws at each end into the side battens [F]. Cut and fix the central support. The rear screws will have to be fixed at an angle [G], the front screws fixed in the normal way. To add extra strength, use PVA glue at the fixing points. The shelf width may determine how many central cross supports you need, and this is where the term ladder frame is derived from. Quite simply, the wider the shelf, the more central cross supports you need, so that the structure resembles a ladder.

Cut the shelf board to size, measuring from the front of the shelf to the wall, then fix with PVA glue and pins – or from

underneath with screws to conceal the fixing positions. Use a couple of fast cramps to hold the board in position during fixing.

Finally, to dress the front edge, use a section of wooden moulding, glued and pinned or screwed from underneath the shelf for concealed fixing [H].

TOMMY'S TIP

To stiffen and strengthen a shelf, attach a batten or metal strip to its front underside. This will generally reinforce the shelf and will prevent it from sagging under heavy weights.

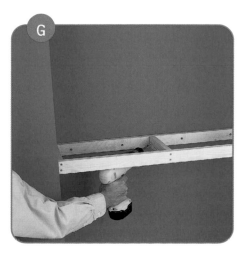

ASSEMBLING FLATPACKS

'Flatpack assembly'. These words used to make me go into a deep depression. 'One learns from one's mistakes doesn't one?' – well, I've made enough of those in the past, so let me pass on some of the things I have learnt about flatpacks over the years.

Firstly, opening the box. Stop! Do not rip it apart – take a craft knife and carefully slit the sticky tape (not the box). Why? Well, unfortunately you may well be taking one or two boxes back to the store, because they contain the wrong components! I often wonder whether the packer has had a bad day and mixes the contents around for revenge or a laugh! So, do not damage the packaging or, even worse, throw it away. This is definitely not a good move until you have finished building the whole project. Quite often the instructions are stuck to the packaging somewhere that you hadn't noticed before you threw it away, or in my case, burnt all the packaging waste on an open fire in the garden! Neither do I want you to lose any sleep over the fact that when you

have finished assembling the complete unit, you end up with more screws and fixings than you had when you started!

I have found all manner of things in some of these fixing kits, and have spent hours reading the burnt remains of an instruction manual, trying in vain to recognize a particular part, desperately looking for a hole or some clue as to where it fits. However, sometimes I can only conclude that the person who packed that box must be moonlighting between jobs – one for B&Q and the other for Ann Summers – because there was obviously an enormous cock up somewhere!

The best tip I can give you concerning any flatpack assembly is not to rush into the construction process – sit down with a cup of tea and familiarize yourself with the instructions and all the different components properly. I don't mean give them just a cursory glance: read the instructions again and again; break them down into digestible bites, and identify and understand each component and fixing. Also, make sure that you have all the parts on the checklist before you start.

In ideal conditions, working from a bench is the best way to build flatpacks. Failing that, create a large clear space on a hard floor, as shown here.

These are two common flat pack assemblies – a wooden upright storage system (a shelf unit) and a kitchen base unit. A shelf system is very simple to assemble and a good way to start your DIY apprenticeship. Attach two of the uprights to the top and bottom shelves with the screws supplied, through the pre-drilled pilot holes [A]. Turn the shelving system over and attach the remaining two uprights as above [B]. Next, simply insert the remaining shelves to the desired height and screw through the pre-drilled positions. Turn the

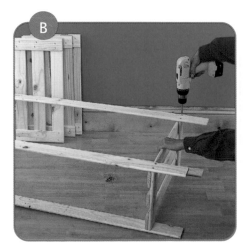

Tools Required:

Tools required
Cordless screwdriver
Pliers
Hammers
Spirit level
Tape measure

shelving system over and screw the shelves tight.

Stand the shelf system upright and secure it to the wall to prevent the unit from falling over if knocked [C].

Nearly all kitchen flatpacks are simply slight variations on a theme! Here, I'm demonstrating how to put together a bog-standard 500mm (19³/₄in) base unit. Open up and assemble one unit at a time, then fit them all together to make up your kitchen. Next, fit the worktops and, finally, hang the doors.

Lay the side panel face down onto the bench or floor. Apply PVA glue to the dowels and tap them home [D]. Also screw in the special connecting bolts, top and bottom where indicated. Repeat this process for the second panel.

The bottom panel and top connecting rails have pre-drilled fixing positions for the connecting bolt locking nuts. There is an indicator arrow on the locking nut. Ensure the arrow points to the outer edge [E]. Apply glue to the dowels, place end panels and connecting rails into position and tighten the bolts [F]. Connect the second side panel by the same method.

To fix the back panel, first run a small bead of glue the length of both slots and slide the back panel into position. Carefully drill two pilot holes into the top rail and secure with two 15mm (⅝in) screws. Wipe off excess glue with a damp cloth.

Turn the cabinet upside down and fix the adjustable legs, by screwing the four plastic lugs with three screws in each lug. Finally screw in the adjustable legs [G]. Turn the cabinet onto its legs. Check for plumbness with a spirit level. Insert shelf supports at the required height, tilt and slide in the shelf [H].

TOMMY'S TIP

Always read the instructions supplied with flatpacks thoroughly before you begin assembling them. Never throw instructions away before you have completed the job — you may live to regret it!

ADAPTING A CUPBOARD FOR MORE STORAGE SPACE

We all realize the importance of space, so adapting existing unused space like lofts, airing cupboards and simple cupboards under the stairs could (with some simple modifications) create the ideal solution for extra storage. Garages! I bet at least half those people across the country lucky enough to have a garage, don't even park their car in it. It's just a storage area for someday-useable items and a lot of junk! Re-organise that space so that you can store what you want, and still park the car. Make a shower room out of the airing cupboard, or a downstairs loo out of the understairs cupboard!

Many years ago in my first little house, there was an understairs cupboard, which opened onto the living room area. My girlfriend wanted to buy a sun bed! It was the early Eighties, and I was concerned about the technology at the time, so I said 'NO! Not in our house', and was surprised at her apparently quiet submission.

Friday nights in the building trade is traditionally known as 'Music Night', and we builders generally meet up for a drink. This particular Friday night though, something had aroused my suspicion, so I decided to call in at the house before I went to meet the boys. I pulled up outside and knocked on the door. No answer! I fetched my keys from the truck, unlocked the door but couldn't get in! I used a bit of pressure and pushed the door open – and there in the hallway in an open box was this great big sun bed!

Well, I was a tad infuriated and called out to my girlfriend – still no answer! I searched the house, to no avail. With only one place left to look, I opened the understairs door and there she was, sitting in the cupboard. She just looked up at me and smiled. I left without saying anything, but started to really giggle as I drove off – all of which goes to show that even a cupboard can be converted to a place of self-induced incarceration!

As if you need to ask! Of course she kept the sun bed. When I asked for an explanation, she said she had intended to hide the sun bed in the spare room where I would never have noticed it. But when it was delivered, it was too heavy for her to move on her own, so she was waiting for her friends to arrive when I turned up! The cupboard simply seemed like the best place to hide at the time.

Decide what you need to store in the cupboard, measure out the space [A] and draw it onto a piece of paper, carefully dividing the space into sections for efficient storage.

Fix a softwood batten to the underside of the stairs and a second one to the floor to fix the partition panel onto [B]. Pre-drill the panels and countersink the screws. Add a bead of PVA glue for extra strength. Ensure that the partition is level using either a spirit level [C], or a plumb line.

To create one or more shelves in the space, fit the required number of battens to both sides using a level to ensure that they match. The shelves and panels can be

TOMMY'S TIP

When adapting a space like this, it's useful to think about the shape and size of the items you wish to store. For example, if you're planning to put the vacuum cleaner in there, measure all of the dimensions of the appliance, and create a space or section that it will fit. That way, you can maximize the storage potential.

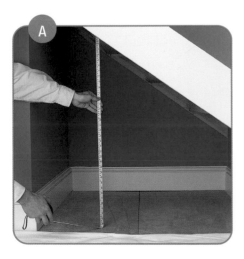

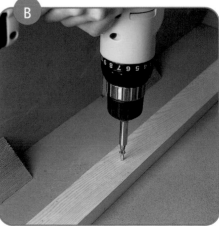

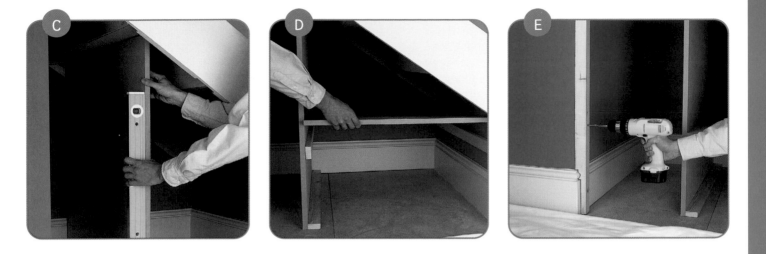

made of MDF or any other timber sheet material – a minimum of 18mm (³/₄in) thick [D]. Additional strength can be added to the shelf by fitting a batten underneath the front edge of the shelf and a batten fitted to the back wall of the cupboard.

Using 50 x 50mm (2 x 2in) PAR, cut and fit two side rails to the cupboard; take care to scribe over the skirting, if the skirting is to remain. Fix with plugs and screws [E].

Use 50 x 25mm (2 x 1in) PAR for the remaining top and bottom rails of the frame, and screw these to the underside of the stairs and the floor [F].

Cut a piece of MDF, plywood or block board to the shape of the opening to form the door. Simple flush hinges can be used to hang the door [G], as it is a cupboard door which will be subject to only infrequent use.

Simply fit a doorknob and a pair of magnetic catches to complete the job [H]. If the finish is too plain, add a pine moulding to form panels on the door before you begin painting it. The panel moulding shape should be drawn onto the door first. Cut to suit the drawn shape, using a jigsaw for any shapes involving curves, and then glue the moulding onto the door using a powerful adhesive. Allow everything to dry thoroughly before painting the door to finish the job.

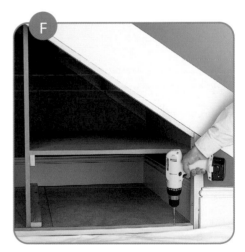

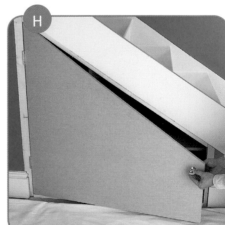

Tools Required:

Measuring tape
Saw
Square
Spirit level
Drill
**Masonry and wood
drill bits**
Hammer
Screwdriver

Adapting a Cupboard for More Storage Space

INSTALLING SLIDING WARDROBE DOORS

As you can imagine, being one of six kids did not afford me much room, even though we lived in a large terraced house. So, as soon as I was old enough, I was keen to move out. When I acquired my first house, which was completely derelict, I sort of bought it with my girlfriend without telling my parents that I had bought it with her... but I also didn't say I hadn't bought it with her, if you know what I mean! I did a huge amount of work restoring this little place.

Although it was only a small two-bedroom terraced house, I wanted it to be really special. When it came to the master bedroom, (I use that term very loosely!), which was about 60cm (2ft) larger than the small bedroom, I wanted to create an illusion of a much larger room as well as utilizing the space available. I selected a set of sliding bi-folding mirror doors, floor-to-ceiling in height and wall-to-wall in width, incorporating the chimneybreast within the wardrobe. The quality of these doors was superb and they really looked the part. Maybe because of the quality, the doors were extremely heavy, and quite an ambitious project for me to fit. I think the doors were designed for a more substantial property than our little place, because once I had fitted them, they would stick sometimes. This was very irritating, especially when my girlfriend called out to me time and again, 'those doors YOU fitted are sticking again!'

Telling this story reminds me of when my Mum came round to have a look at the finished house, and the traumatic afternoon I spent waiting for the opportune moment to say 'Mum, I'm not coming home any more!' Bear in mind that my Mum's a strict Catholic, so I sort of blurted it out at speed. This statement was followed by a protracted silence, broken only by me saying 'would you like to have a look around the house?' It was only when we entered the bedroom and were facing the wall-to-wall, floor-to-ceiling mirror wardrobes that I saw the expression on Mum's face (reflected in the blooming mirror!) as to why I had made the decision to move in! Can you imagine trying to explain to a strict Catholic Irish mother that the floor to ceiling, wall-to-wall mirrored wardrobes positioned opposite the bed (a double one!) was purely for suitable storage and to create the illusion of a larger room? No! Well, I didn't try either....

Quite a range of sliding wardrobe door systems are available as a package, as are independent track systems for various standard doors, or even for creating a custom-made design of your own. What I am going to show you is how to fit a very simple door and track package that works an absolute treat.

Using a tape measure and pencil, mark the dimensions of the wardrobe on the walls and ceiling with the aid of a spirit level [A]. The minimum internal depth of the wardrobe should be 600mm (24in) and the floor to ceiling height should be 2286mm (90in). If your ceiling height is more than 90in it will be necessary to build an infill down from the ceiling to obtain

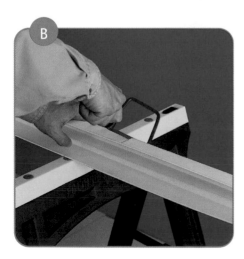

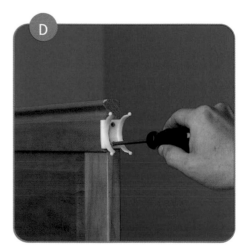

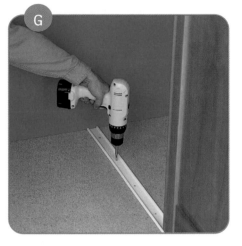

the 90in overall height. Do not attempt to raise the bottom track above floor level.

Cut the ceiling and floor tracks to the required opening width to ensure flush alignment with the end walls [B]. Skirting boards can be cut to allow the doors to close against the wall, or alternatively fit a batten to the wall. Fix the ceiling track securely, preferably through the ceiling into the ceiling joists, but if this is not practicable use proper plasterboard fixings [C]. When fixing the ceiling track, remember to allow for 10mm ($^3/_8$in) fascia thickness in your calculations. Using the screwdriver, fix the top guides to the doors with the screws provided, as shown on the end rails [D].

Position the rear door first, by placing the top of the door into the rear guide of the top track. This is achieved by angling the door into the top track with the bottom of the door held away from the bottom track [E]. When the top guides are in position, place the bottom of the door onto the bottom track rear guide. Use a spirit level against the door to ensure the accurate positioning of the bottom track [F]. With the bottom track perfectly in line, simply fix with the screws provided [G].

Cut the timber fascia to the required length. Clean the front face of the ceiling track with a solvent (white spirit) and allow it to dry. Carefully remove the backing paper from the fascia adhesive tape, and then press the fascia board onto the ceiling track face, applying pressure along the length for good adhesion [H].

TOMMY'S TIP

If you're a big bloke like me, ensure you leave enough room to fit the shoulders of your clothes within the wardrobe and fit the rails so that your trousers and shirts don't drag on the floor.

Tools Required:

Drill
Hacksaw
Tenon saw
Screwdriver
Spirit level
Tape measure
Hammer

FITTING CURTAIN RAILS AND POLES

When people say to me that they are having real problems fitting curtain rails and poles in their property, I don't say 'Oh why? It's such a simple job': I can actually sympathize. Just think about it logically, which is the way to approach the job in all buildings. A window must have support directly above it, spanning the width of the opening, because if you build the brick wall on top of the window, it would obviously collapse. In older period properties an arch would be built on the outside to perform the support function, and there would be a large piece of timber (wall plate) on the inside, which the window would be fixed to. This would be plastered over to cover it, but it would make fixing curtain rails and poles a bit easier, as they would be fixed directly into the wood. However, with later houses, the timber wall plates were replaced with impenetrable concrete lintels, and steel catnic lintels. For the amateur DIY person, this may present what might appear to be an insurmountable problem and I have had to mount many rescue missions for friends and family. It all boils down to a bit of careful planning, and testing what is above the window, so that you know which fixings to purchase. If the top of the window is very tight to the ceiling, it may be possible to fit the curtain pole or track to the ceiling to hang the curtains on. However, if you use plasterboard fixings for the curtain rails, remember that they may not be strong enough to take the weight of heavy curtains and you may have to locate the ceiling joists.

The most common position for fixing curtain rails and poles is directly above the window. If you are fixing into masonry, you must use the hammer setting on your drill with the appropriate size masonry bit to suit the rawl plugs. It is very important that the fixings are made into the masonry and not just the plaster. This may be particularly difficult if you are fixing into a concrete or steel lintel. It may be far more practical to fix a piece of 25mm (1in) thick planed timber above the window first, painted to match the wall colour, then attach the pole or rail fixings to it.

If you are not happy with the appearance of the pole or rail, you could always create and fix a pelmet to hide it, and perhaps cover the pelmet with some of the curtaining material. Whatever you do though, don't let it drive you up the pole!

FIXING A POLE

A wooden pole will come with two ring type brackets, which the pole is threaded through. The rings will fit into round wall fixings, which will have holes through the middle to fix them to the wall. Firstly, establish a point above the head of the window where you would like your curtains to hang from, say 100mm (4in). Mark the line with a straight piece of wood and spirit level. Now mark a point at the centre of the window. Having established your line, you should decide where you want your fixings along the pole. Measure the pole then divide the distance by four. Measure the distance one side of the centre and mark. Repeat for the other side and you have your fixing points.

Remember, your screws should be long enough to fix right into the masonry as well as the plaster, plus the depth of the fixing hole in the ring fixing. Drill your holes and insert plugs. Fix the round wall fixings to the wall [A].

Next, fit the wood support ring to the wall fixing, using screws to secure one to the other [B]. Remember to thread

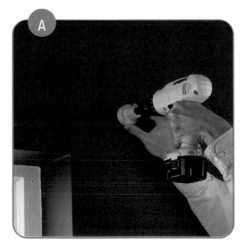

TOMMY'S TIP

Whenever you are fixing curtain rails or poles, be sure to use a ladder or stepladder. Never be tempted to stand on a chair; it might be the last time you do!

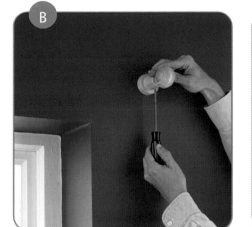

Tools Required:

Drill
Masonry bit
Plugs and screws
Steel self-tapping screws
Spirit level

the pole through the rings first and don't forget also to thread the curtain rings onto the pole, spacing these at a suitable distance along the length of the pole. Lastly, you can fit the end stops to the pole, securing with the small screws supplied [C].

FIXING A CURTAIN TRACK

When you buy a rail it will usually come with enough fixing brackets for its length. So the number of brackets will establish the spacing along the track. Measure the length of the track and if necessary cut to suit the window first. As for the pole, the same applies to the track. Mark a level line at a suitable point above the window head to hang your curtains.

Screw each bracket along your line [D]. The track will snap over the brackets, starting at the top and working from one end [E]. Having fixed the rail, you can now slip the gliders along the track. Push and screw the end stop gliders into place [F].

Some curtain tracks have an integral cord pull fitted (far right in the illustration), to assist the closing of curtains.

Wooden curtain poles feature decorative finials at their ends and are a good choice for a more aesthetic look.

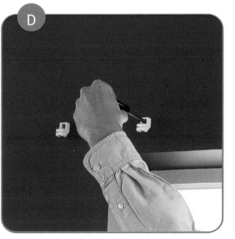

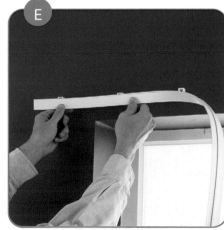

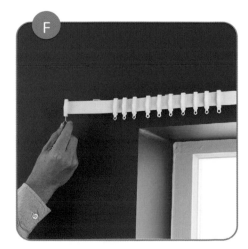

I often look in amazement at the end result of people's efforts to get something to work – take hanging pictures for instance. My own mother prefers to hang her collection of photographs, all individually framed, across the whole of the three walls of the lounge, leaving only the huge window uncovered. Now I have said to Mum, what about if I make a montage of pictures on a huge back panel, framed like a big picture, then hang it in the lounge? It would leave you plenty of wall space for anything else you might want to display... My real worry was that Mum might find an electric cable with one of the many fixings knocked into the wall, but nevertheless I was told in no uncertain terms what I could do with my montage.

I'm not sure whether this behaviour is typical of all mothers, but my mother-in-law has exactly the same fetish for a hammer and nails. Maybe knocking nails into a wall proves to be therapeutic for mothers, although the look my mother-in-law gives me sometimes, I'm sure she could think of a place far more therapeutic (for her) to whack the nails into! Seriously though, be careful. Check for cables before you start and use some of the purpose-made fixtures for picture hanging.

None of us are exempt from mini-disasters and they always seem to happen at the most inconvenient times. During a private contract, refurbishing a very damp basement flat, on a really short time scale (the story of my life), we worked around the clock to get the job completed before Christmas. On Christmas Eve I wanted to be finished with work by 1pm, to enable the lads and myself to participate in the annual festivities – carol singing and the like! At 12.30pm everything was going like clockwork, when the client asked if we could possibly fix a special unit in the alcove. We grudgingly agreed. Willie drilled the last hole into the return wall, and BANG! – a big blue flash and all the lights and power went out! Talk about 'Sod's Law' – some plonker had run a power cable diagonally across a wall to feed a socket on a completely different wall. Half an inch either way and we would have missed it. By the time we had repaired, re-plastered and redecorated the damage, we arrived at our local prayer meeting past closing time...!

MAKING A PICTURE FRAME

To give a print or picture a bit of something extra, use a mounting card, maybe in a contrasting colour. This method is particularly useful if you wish to make the picture itself become the focal point. The eye is naturally drawn in to the artwork. Cut the mounting card to the overall size you want, and mark out the section that you wish to remove to allow as much of the picture to be revealed as you want. This cut-out is achieved by using a bevel-mount cutter, or alternatively a flat metal square and a craft knife [A]. You can also purchase ready-cut mounts from any picture supplier.

Using a mitre saw (or a tenon saw and mitre box) cut the picture frame section to suit your card size, allowing for external mitres at the end of each piece in your calculations [B]. Glue and pin the four sections together; there are special corner-angled staples available to connect the sections together [C]. Position the glass, mounting card with picture taped in place, and the backing (which can be cut from hardboard), then tap in the spring frame clips [D].

Use a bradawl to make the holes in the back of the frame for screwing in the eyelets [E] and connect the string or picture wire to the eyelets to mount your artwork on a picture hook.

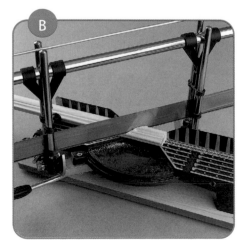

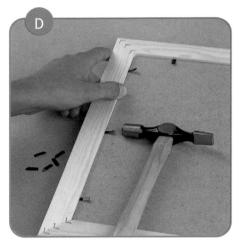

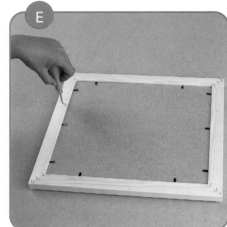

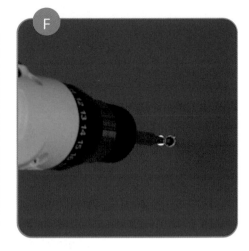

If you are attempting to hang an extremely heavy piece of artwork, or maybe a tapestry wall hanging, the fixing will have to be substantial. Carefully decide on the hanging position. Using a hammer drill and masonry bit [F] (the masonry bit must match the rawl plug size), use either a conventional screw with a minimum length of 50mm (2in) with about 25 percent of its total length protruding to hang the artwork on, or a heavy duty hook screwed into the rawl plug to ensure that your Mona Lisa stays exactly where you want her.

For average-weight pictures and prints, conventional picture hooks with masonry pins are available from any DIY store or picture-framing suppliers, and these are fixed by tapping them gently into the wall with a hammer [G].

Modern plastic hooks with four smaller pins for fixing are available as an alternative to hooks and pins. These can be bought from any hardware or DIY store and are fixed in the same way as conventional hooks [H].

HANGING MIRRORS

Fixing mirrors can be achieved in two ways – either by using a special adhesive or by driving mirror screws into rawl plugs. The supplier should make any fixing holes in the mirror. Do not attempt to do this yourself.

Remember, the quality of the finished job will undoubtedly reflect upon your perceived ability as an expert DIYer – or not!

TOMMY'S TIP

Only hang mirrors if you are attractive! Seriously though, make sure that your fixing can take the weight of your mirror: some have mouldings and surrounds which can be very heavy.

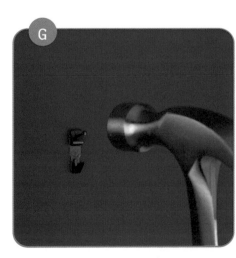

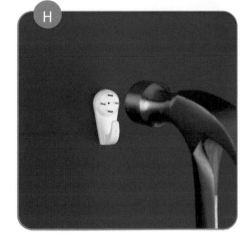

Tools Required:

Tape measure
Flat steel square
Hammer
Mitre saw (tenon saw and mitre block)
Hammer drill
Masonry bits
Craft knife
Bradawl
Wire cutters or pliers

95

REPLACING KITCHEN CUPBOARD DOORS

You happen to be sitting in the waiting room of the doctor's surgery – you have an appointment and you're on time so you don't bring a newspaper with you. Looking around the room in amazement at the other 25 people there, you're inclined to ask, 'Well, what time was their appointment then?!' After twiddling your thumbs for half an hour and only two people have been in to see the doctor, you begin to wonder at all the coughing and spluttering, whether you're going to leave the doctor's with a worse condition than you went in with!

To distract yourself from these thoughts, you pick up a magazine, carefully checking the inside cover for any contagious diseases. Looking down the features sections, you notice that Elton John has a full head of hair (I mean real hair!), and you immediately look at the front cover again to check the date. As you suspected, the magazine is almost as old as you are. You look around and sigh; realizing that looking at the magazine is better than the alternative.

All these glossy magazines are the same: enticing you; encouraging you to spend all your hard earned cash on double-glazing! Or now there's even treble glazing! Or maybe you need a lovely mock Victorian conservatory in beautiful white UPVC plastic. Then there's the wonderful new fitted kitchens in all sorts of lovely wood and paint finishes at a price you would have to sell half your house to afford!

Now that doesn't have to be the case, because the majority of kitchen carcasses are made in a very similar manner from very similar materials, and providing your units are in a sound condition and you are happy with the layout, you can achieve a great transformation by changing the doors and drawer fronts. To make that change spectacular, change the worktops and sink, add some nice lighting and redecorate the kitchen. A transformation that would even impress the likes of Carol Smiley and Laurence Llewelyn Bowen from 'Changing Rooms', and also wouldn't mean cancelling your annual holiday for the next ten years!

The kitchen I built in my first house, I built in brick. I had to make all the doors and drawers myself. Rather than change that kitchen, I decided to move! Here's how you can make a change without moving.

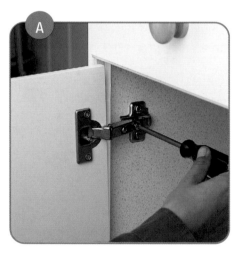

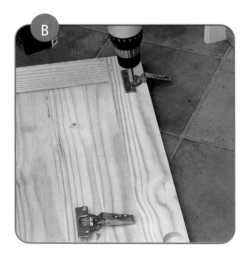

Using a slotted or crosshead screwdriver, undo the door hinges leaving in place the hinge plates attached to the unit [A]. The replacement doors normally have the hinge holes pre-cut. If not, the holes can be cut quite easily using a circular hinge-cutter, which simply fits into the end of your drill.

Replacement hinges are readily available from DIY stores and hardware shops. Transfer the hinges from the old door, and fit them to the new door with the two fixing screws [B]. Use a bradawl to start the screw holes.

Offer the new door to the unit, and screw the hinge in place on the hinge plate via the large central screw [C]. The second

Tools Required:

Screwdriver
Tape measure
Square
Drill
Wood bits
Cramp
Circular hinge-cutter
Bradawl

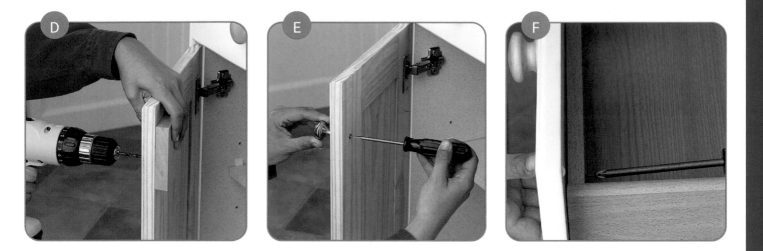

screw is for adjustment only, to align the door to the unit. Repeat this process for the bottom hinge. Hey presto! A new door!

Replace the door handles by marking the position and drilling through to attach the handle. To avoid breakout occurring when you drill through the door, temporarily attach a block of wood to the door behind the drilling point with a cramp [D].

Simply hold the handle and screw in the threaded bolt [E]. If the bolt is a touch on the short side, countersink the hole a bit on the inside of the door to allow the bolt to protrude a little further out.

Swapping over kitchen drawer fronts is a very simple process. Firstly, remove the old drawer front by undoing the two retaining screws located inside the drawer [F]. Attach the new drawer handle, by drilling a hole through the centres of the drawer front [G]. Countersink the hole a little bit on the back

of the drawer front to prevent the bolt head from protruding out of the edge of the drawer when it has been attached.

Attaching the new drawer front is achieved by screwing through the two fixing points, into the back face of the drawer front. Repeat this process on all the units, watch your kitchen gradually becoming transformed, and reward yourself for a job well done!

TOMMY'S TIP

Use a bradawl to make mini pilot holes and a guide for your drill bit before you begin drilling. Also, if you are using a hinge-cutter for the first time, practice thoroughly on a piece of waste wood before you attempt the new door. It could save you making a mess of things.

REALIGNING KITCHEN CUPBOARD DOORS/STICKING DRAWERS

This job really can be a curse. What I advise is to look carefully at how the door hinge of a unit works and consider exactly how much adjustment is actually possible. Thankfully, there is a considerable amount of adjustment in most types of hinge these days.

Very recently (within the past year or so), my workmate Willie and I had to fit a kitchen to an old Grade II listed building that we were restoring. The kitchen was a mass-produced standard kitchen in the Shaker style, from a big national supplier, and it was very nice. We adapted it slightly by making our own pelmets, cornices and skirtings and then we fitted granite worktops to it.

The doors and drawer fronts are always the last things to be fitted in a new kitchen, but try as I might I just could not get the doors to sit quite right. It wasn't until I looked along the length of the kitchen, that I saw some of the doors were curled like bananas. The supplier, who shall remain nameless, sent somebody to check out my grievance, and apparently the problem had occurred during storage. He didn't say whether it was storage under their supervision or ours!

The company generously supplied a set of replacement doors, which weren't much better than the first lot. With patience and persistence, and a little splash of compromise thrown in, we finally managed to align all the doors and drawers perfectly (well almost)!

As with the rest of the house, it's a very good idea to give your kitchen a major overhaul every now and then. Don't let things go too far or the problem may go beyond repair.

I recommend that you service the kitchen once a year – a good spring clean, if you like. Give the units a really thorough cleaning. Apply a drop of lubricating oil to the hinges, tighten up all the handles, and repair any damage or scratches to the cabinets. Replace any badly damaged footboards (skirtings) and service any appliances as required.

TOMMY'S TIP

Use a packer for spacing cupboard doors – it makes it much easier to keep spaces consistent. Also, when you are adjusting a drawer front, re-drill new fixing holes, rather than using the existing ones. This ensures that the drawer front stays in the desired position.

Making adjustments to the doors of your kitchen units is an easy and simple operation. Most standard mass-produced kitchens are supplied with plumb hinges. These are hinges that are cut into the back face of the door, spring-loaded to fit over a hinge plate that's attached to the cabinet itself. Constant opening and closing over a period of time can cause the doors to drop out of alignment, hence the need to make adjustments.

There are three areas of door adjustment on a cabinet hinge. The first is the large central screw that you use to attach the door to the cabinet. This screw tightens down over a slot, which will allow the door to be adjusted away from the cabinet if the door is binding (rubbing) [A].

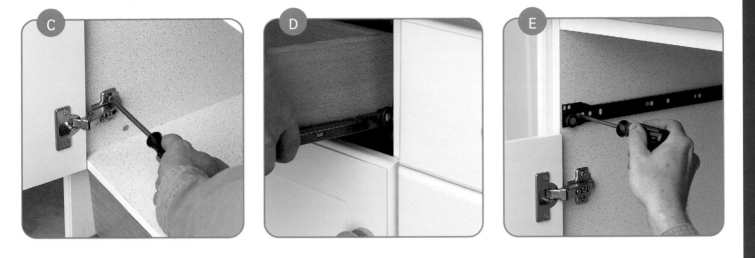

Adjustment number two is made by tightening or loosening the smaller fixed screw, located next to the first screw mentioned above. This adjusts the door to the left or right of the cabinet (as you look at it) when closed, allowing you to centralize and equally space the doors apart [B].

The third area of adjustment is on the hinge plate that's attached to the cabinet. This plate has a vertical slot, which allows the door to be raised or lowered to align with the cabinet and the other doors [C]. The clever part about all this is that all you need to make these adjustments is a cross-head screwdriver.

To adjust a drawer (not just the drawer front), first remove the drawer from the unit by extending the drawer right out, then lift the front of the drawer to free the drawer from the runners [D].

Make a few pencil marks on the unit to show the existing position and the proposed new position. Unscrew the runners and reposition [E]. Use a cramp to hold the runner in position temporarily, to allow for new pilot holes to be drilled [F]

before securing with screws. When you are piloting holes, remember only drill to half the screw's length, using a drill bit which is slightly narrower than the screw you are using.

If the drawer runs perfectly but its front rubs on a door or worktop as it closes, you may be able to solve the problem by simply unscrewing the front from the drawer, repositioning the drawer front and screwing it back together again [G].

SOLID WOOD UNITS

Drawer units that work on wooden battens as runners need an occasional rubbing over with candle wax along the runner and drawer base. This well help to ensure smooth and effortless operation.

To remove greasy finger marks and grime from wooden doors and drawer fronts, use a solution of vinegar – it works a treat.

Tools Required:

Cross-head screwdriver
Sandpaper
Drill
Drill bits
Cramp
Candle wax (optional)

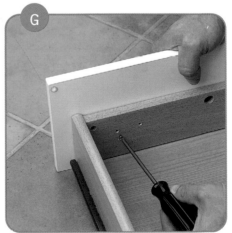

REPAIRING/ OVERHAULING WINDOWS

Windows are a subject of national debate. Should you keep the originals – that is, those actually designed for the building – or replace them with double-glazed windows?

I think my opinions are well known on the subject! I will concede that there are certain cases where double-glazing is justified, but I can think of much better ways of spending thousands of pounds of my hard-earned cash! In most cases, the original window design is the one best suited to the building for a number of reasons. If the original windows need replacing it's probably only because some aspect of basic maintenance has been ignored. If you do replace the windows in your house, consider replacing like for like.

It was partly due to works of this nature that I ended up on television. Whilst refurbishing a large Victorian property in Hampstead for an executive producer, which included over-hauling all the windows, I was asked to appear on television. I think that one of the reasons for the invitation may have been due to the light-hearted approach myself, my workmates and my Dad had towards our work. My Dad, although nearly ten years retired at the time, loved coming to work with me and Willie and the lads, purely for 'the crack' (Irish terminology for fun and wind-ups!).

Dad was a stickler for break times. First break at 11am, lunch break at 1pm and last break, tea at three! One day, unbeknown to Dad, a very good friend of mine, Richard, was carrying out a contract, creating a large loft apartment directly in front of us, a couple of streets away. So high was this loft apartment that Richard could see where we were working. Every day during tea at three, he would drop his strides, reverse out of the big picture window and moon at my Dad from afar. My Dad wasn't one to swear much, but tea at three became the exception. Of course we all knew! But straight-faced we would be, aghast at this behaviour until one day after the moon, Richard turned around and revealed his face. My Dad had great vision (in more ways than one) – disbelief at first, then the realization of the wind up, as it dawned on him that we had been in on it for days.

It may be a long-winded way of saying it, but if the 'window of opportunity' comes your way, grab it, as there are no rehearsals in this life!

Although my personal preference is for box frame and sash windows, the most commonly used window in this country is the casement window. This type of window is particularly vulnerable to the weather, simply because they are normally face-fixed (flush with the brickwork) and thus have no protection from the weather. The opening sash often distorts slightly with the weather, causing it to rattle and become draughty. One simple solution may be to move the catch plate of the lever fastener, to pull the sash tighter into the frame so preventing the rattle and reducing the draught.

Undo the catch plate from its original position on the mullion or transom and move it slightly away from the sash [A]. Hold the catch plate in its new position, use a bradawl to start off the new fixing holes [B], insert the screws and secure. Having moved the catch plate slightly, when the window is closed, the rattle should now be squeezed out.

Sticking windows can be quite a problem if they are left undecorated. A window will quickly let in moisture, which will make the timber swell, in turn making the window difficult to open and close. When a window sticks, a lot of people force the window either open or shut. You have to be careful when doing this, because forcing the window can break the mortice and tenon joints in the sash construction.

Tools Required:

Screwdriver
Bradawl
Hammer
Craft knife
Plane
Sandpaper
Candle wax

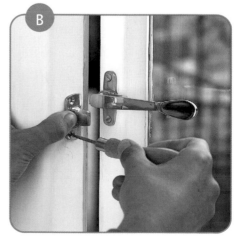

First, use candle wax on both the sash window edge and the mullion or transom edge [C]. If that doesn't work, you may have to plane the edge of the sash to allow the window to operate efficiently [D]. Keep attempting to open and close the window whilst planing, to ensure you remove only the minimum amount.

After planing the edge, it is imperative that you prime, undercoat and topcoat the raw edge as soon as possible [E]. Allow the paint to dry fully between coats, and then rub up with wax.

SASH WINDOWS

Ensure sash cords are replaced when broken, and always replace all the cords to the whole window when replacing one! Ensure that the windows are always well decorated, especially the sill section, which is particularly vulnerable to the weather. When replacing a pane of glass, don't forget to paint over the putty, when it's dry.

STRING
CORD
CUT HERE
NAIL HERE

Refitting window sashes: [1] Mark the cord grooves [2] Pull the cord through [3] Cut the cords at mark [4] Nail the cord to the sash.

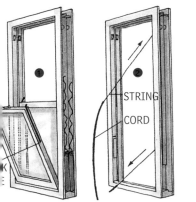

TOMMY'S TIP

Never, ever paint a window in the closed position. After painting a window in the OPEN position, move the sashes after a couple of hours to ensure that the window doesn't stick. If the windows are stuck, it may be necessary to use a craft knife to carefully break the paint seal. Always remove all window furniture before painting.

REPAIRING/ OVERHAULING DOORS

A lot of people put off repairing, overhauling or replacing doors because they think it's a difficult job. However, you leave the repairs at your peril, because before long the damage to the door will be beyond repair and it will require replacing. And the original cause of the problem will still need to be addressed!

I'll briefly outline a few of the potential problems. Firstly, you've had new carpets fitted and the doors are binding over the carpet; not only do you damage the new carpet, but there is huge pressure exerted on the joints, which can break or weaken the door considerably. Secondly, any door that's not properly fitted, which is sticking or binding, is a problem. Thirdly, slamming the door or forcing the door closed will put pressure on the joints, resulting in permanent damage to the door. This will also loosen or damage the frame, which in turn damages the plasterwork, which means repairs and redecorating. See what I mean about dealing with the problem straight away – you can avoid wasting a lot of time and expense!

STICKING DOORS

With the onset of winter and damp conditions, doors may possibly start to stick along the side and bottom and could need 'easing'. Before you do any remedial work, first check that the hinges are not worn or broken. If the door rocks a bit when pushed and pulled, this is normally a sign that the hinges are worn. Replace them immediately.

Let's start with a side-sticking door, provided the hinges are sound. Close the door tightly and mark a pencil line down the edge against the jamb [A]. You will now see where the door needs easing back from the high points along the pencil line. You can now use a hand plane to plane off the high points until the edge is the same distance from the pencil line all the way down [B].

Shut the door once more and using a flat piece of wood, say a piece of hardboard for instance, scribe a line on the bottom of the door [C]. This will show where you have any tight points on the floor. Remove the door from its hinges and plane off any points.

In some instances you may have to adjust the hinges on the door in order to square it to the frame for a good fit. Alternatively, you may need to pack the hinges out if they have been cut in too deep, making the door bind on the frame. Remove the door and hinges [D] by wedging the door underneath with small wedges to support it in the open position. Now cut small packers from thin card [E] and place the card packer behind the hinges [F] and screw back into position. This will adjust your door towards the jamb. You may need one or two pieces of card, depending on the amount of adjustment required. Screw the hinge(s) back into position, just one screw per hinge whilst you close the door to check. Add or remove

Tools Required:

Plane
Pencil
Hammer
Chisel
Screwdriver

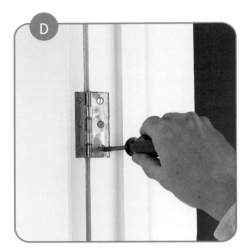

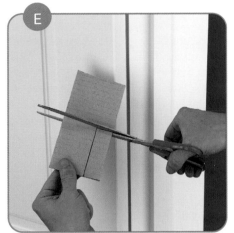

pieces of card until you have the right combination for a perfect square fit and no binding, then fix the rest of the screws.

If you have a rattling door, this means the door is not meeting the stop or jamb correctly, therefore you will need to remove and replace the jamb in a new position to make a nice snug fit.

Take a hammer and chisel and gently tap the joint between jamb and frame to ease the jamb off, using a piece of wood to lever against and ease the jamb away from the frame (this prevents any damage caused by the lever). Remove all nails or just hammer back to the face of the wood for re-fixing. Now close the door. Re-fix the vertical jamb first to allow the door to close firmly but snugly [G] and then the other vertical jamb followed by the top jamb for a nice rattle-free door. Job done! I used a folded piece of sandpaper between the door and the jamb as a spacer, which will allow for coats of paint, and no binding.

STRENGTHENING A HINGE

Quite often a common problem occurs when a door has been taken off and re-fixed a few times. The screws loosen within the fixing holes, and the door doesn't operate properly (this can also be a cause of a door sticking or binding). The problem is simply solved by paring down some softwood into dowels. Add PVA wood glue and tap the dowels into the old holes. When the glue has gone off, cut off the excess dowel and re-fix the hinges.

TOMMY'S TIP

There are various ways of cutting out for hinges on a new door. You can use a router and jig, but I use a hammer and chisel with a special hinge cutter. The cutter is simply a template, and comes in various sizes.

REPLACING DOOR FURNITURE

There has always been a vast range of door furniture to choose from, but the golden rule is to buy good quality fittings. I would always advise somebody against buying cheap, poor quality door furniture, because it just won't last.

This subject reminds me of a contract we once had to do for a documentary film director. The job involved installing a set of bi-folding mahogany doors in an opening created from a load-bearing spine wall. These doors were hand-made, very heavy and complex to fit, so I asked a very good friend of mine, Richard, an excellent joiner, to help me.

Richard and I decided to hatch a plot against poor Willie, my workmate, but please, don't try this at home! Richard had hidden some theatrical blood in his toolbox and was deliberately manoeuvring his hand very close to the blade of the electric saw. Will kept shouting out, 'Richard, watch your fingers, you'll lose one!' Whilst out getting materials, I went into a trick shop at Richard's request and purchased a joke thumb. It was made of latex, but looked really authentic, with a roughly cut end and red blood attached. I arrived back at the job at nearly lunchtime. I slipped Richard the thumb and went

to make the tea. Richard poured the blood over the saw and blade, some more on the floor, folded his thumb under a dirty old cloth with the false one positioned and held in place by the cloth. He added a good helping of blood all over the cloth and hand, and then shouted for Willie's help. Willie ran in from outside and witnessed Richard pretending to be on the verge of fainting. Willie, bless him, held Richard upright saying, 'Don't look, I'll look for you!' He then half carried, half dragged Richard to the ground floor bathroom to wash the wound. He was calling to me all the time but I couldn't come out for crying with laughter. Will turned on the tap and told Richard not to look. Richard chose this moment to let the thumb drop with a thud into the sink. I heard Willie scream '…. his thumb's fell off! Tommy where are you, start the truck – we must get to the hospital. Tommy, where the **** are you!' I was kneeling on the floor in the kitchen, holding my sides from bursting. Willie still has not forgiven us to this day….

So you see, with new doors opening, you could be furnished with nothing but fun! It all hinges on whether you can handle somebody ringing your bell!

REPLACING A DOOR HANDLE

The first thing to do is to remove the old handle, so, using a screwdriver, remove the four screws holding the handle plate [A]. Remember to remove only one side of the handle plate at a time. Then, place the new handle over the square spindle [B] to check if you need to cut the spindle shorter, in order to allow the new handle plate to sit flat against the door when it has been fitted.

Use the spirit level to check if your new handle plate is level by holding it vertically against the edge of the fitting. Then mark your fixing holes with a bradawl [C] and drill small pilot

TOMMY'S TIP

If you are replacing a door handle, make sure you choose a new one that will cover or re-use the screw holes left behind by the old one. This will save you a re-decorating job and will keep the door looking its best for longer.

holes for the screws [D]. Make sure the holes are just big enough to accept the screw provided with the new handles. Screw the first handle to the door checking with the spirit level [E] and adjusting as you go [F].

Now go to the other side of the door and do exactly the same to fix the other handle.

OILING THE LATCH MECHANISM

It is always a good idea to oil the latch mechanism in the door handle whilst you are in the neighbourhood. To do this,

Tools Required:

Small screwdriver
Small spirit level
Bradawl
Drill

remove both door handles and the spindle, remembering to place something on the floor between the door and the jamb to keep the door ajar. This curious expression always makes me think, 'what have jam jars got to do with open doors?' Where I come from a jam jar stands for a salmon and bloater (motor car) – but that's another story. Anyway, I digress: use a cushion or something soft to wedge the door open – perhaps your partner? – just kidding!

Place a long bladed screwdriver through the hole where the spindle goes, and remove the two holding screws.

Holding the screwdriver either side of the door, give it a firm pull towards the forward edge to free the latch [G]. Having oiled the latch, push it back into position and replace the two fixing screws. Replace the handles as mentioned above. You can now close and open the door with your new handles perfectly attached, remembering of course to remove your partner first!

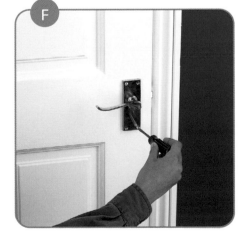

INSTALLING A DOORBELL

Doorbells! I've always preferred 'knockers' myself – you can't beat a good knocker, I say. Knockers normally hang approximately three-quarters of the way up from the floor. I think that's when they look at their best. I particularly like the pear-shaped ones, with a bit of weight to the bottom of them. I find it really helpful for a particularly good banging! A good knocker Is something to be admired, a centrepiece if you like. I've spent many a Sunday morning giving my wife's a good polishing, then buffing up with a soft cloth. I can understand why she doesn't like to do it – the Brasso polish used to make her hands and nails black. But I don't mind, its worthwhile having the cleanest and shiniest knocker in the turning.

Enough about my fetish for knockers – I'm supposed to be telling you about doorbells. Though you have to admit, as a word 'knockers' has more of a ring to it! Not a lot of people know this, but 'knockers' has two meanings where I come from. The first is as I described above – an ornate feature to a front door, as well as a civil means of enquiry. The other – yes, you've probably guessed it – is a term for a person who tries to avoid paying for work or a service. Unfortunately this happens quite a lot in the building industry, sometimes with complete justification. Sometimes being 'knocked' is a reflection of the quality of work!

Thankfully, I haven't suffered being 'knocked' often in my lifetime, but there was this one time when I was a teenager working with my mate Webbie for my Dad. This job was a big front garden landscaping job, in Stamford Hill, London. We were blissfully unaware that it was called the 'small builder's graveyard'.... We excavated six lovely big loads of rubbish and laid a huge area of paving. The job looked beautiful. It was just before Christmas, so it was going to pay for our holiday. When Dad went to get paid, the client said to him, 'Money, what money? I had a dream!' and walked off. Apparently this man had sold his father's house to 32 different young couples, taking deposits off all of them. He 'knocked' all the builders for fortunes, but I think Dad must have made him an offer he couldn't refuse, because we were the only ones to get paid, although we did only receive half. He got seven years for his troubles. Now he was an outrageous knocker, and the best place for him was being 'banged up'.

INSTALLING A WIND-UP DOORBELL

Wind-up doorbells are easy to install, as they require no wiring for electricity. They operate by being wound up (like an old watch – remind you of anyone?), and as the button is pressed, this releases the spring and causes the striker to hit the bell. The downside of this type of doorbell is that they need to be wound up frequently, but take care not to over-wind them as they can then become stuck.

Drill a hole through the door from the outside and push the shaft from the button through to the inside [A]. Screw the button to the door. On the other side, place the underside of the bell over the shaft and screw this into place [B]. Replace the outer cover and wind up [C]. Your bell is ready for action.

Tools Required:

Drill and bit
Screwdriver
Electrical screwdriver
Hammer
Cable cutter
Cable dips

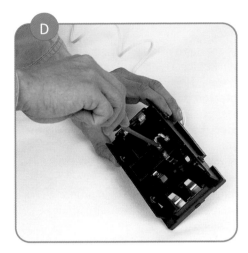

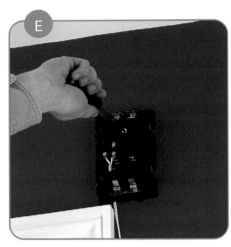

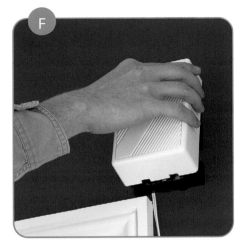

INSTALLING A BATTERY OPERATED DOORBELL

You can install a battery operated doorbell system anywhere near the door, but make sure that you do not situate the unit near a heat source. The battery housing will normally be located within the bell casing, with two terminals for joining to the other end of the wires coming from the doorbell button. It doesn't make any difference which way round you connect the wires to the terminals – either way is fine [D].

Drill a hole through the doorframe ready to take the wire. Fix the battery box to the wall above the door [E], run the wire down the side of the frame and thread it through the hole to the other side. Put the cover of the unit back on [F]. Gently hammer in the cable clips to secure the cable neatly to the frame [G]. Separate the conductors and join each one to the end of the bell terminal [H]. Screw the button fixing into place.

MAINS OPERATED BELLS

Mains operated bells are fitted to the consumer unit via a suitable transformer. The transformer reduces the 240-volt supply down to the required voltage of the bell – anything from 3–12 volts. Carefully follow the installation instructions, ensuring that the 240-volt mains supply cannot bridge and cross over to the low voltage bell push and cable.

TOMMY'S TIP

If the consumer unit is near the front door, wire up a transformer system bell. If there is a considerable distance between the front door and the consumer unit, it may well be worth considering a battery operated doorbell. Me..? Well, I like the wind up, but as I said, you can't beat a lovely knocker!

DOOR SECURITY

Apart from windows, the other major vulnerable security areas are the front and rear doors to your property. I'm well aware that in certain areas crime, particularly burglary, is more prevalent. However, that definitely does not mean that we have just got to accept the inevitability of becoming a victim, because there are certain preventative measures that we can take, which I've aptly named 'odds reducers'!

A few but simple, well-taken preventative measures can reduce your susceptibility to burglary by enormous margins – door security being one of the most valuable.

Securing a front or back door must include all aspects of the door – the frame, the door itself, the glazing, the locks, the KEEPS of the locks, the hinges and the lighting. Ensure that the frame is securely fixed within the masonry. It wouldn't hurt to add a couple of extra frame fixings equally spaced apart to both uprights of the frame. The new chemical fixings now available are exceptionally good. Next thing to check is the door. Check that it is in good condition, and hasn't been weakened by too much cutting down of the rails (the skeleton frame of the door itself). Check that the panels of the door are substantial. Door panels are quite often easily smashed in or removed. You can counteract this risk by fixing a sheet of ply cut to shape and size to the inside of the door with screws. Glass panels can be protected from the inside by detachable fine mesh or ornate metal grilles. Ensure that there is a high level light or vandal-proof low-level light fitted externally to observe clearly who's calling at the door. See below for lots of information about hinge bolts, doorguards, bolts and locks, and finally connect the front door to the alarm system.

Alarm systems are great, provided they're fitted properly, and you don't do what I did in my first house. After I rebuilt this derelict box (the house), which took about 18 months to complete, I finally had the alarm fitted over the weekend then went to work on Monday morning forgetting, of course, to set the alarm. On my return home in the evening from work, I discovered that somebody had used my shovel from the garden to smash through the large but thin plywood panel on the brand new back door to break in. I learnt three lessons that day! Don't leave tools accessible outside, select your main front and rear doors very carefully, and don't forget to turn on your alarm!

FITTING HINGE BOLTS AND DOOR GUARDS

Fitting hinge bolts is a relatively simple job. It's a good idea to fit at least two bolts per door – basically, the more you have, the more secure your door will be. Open the door and drill a hole on the inside of the door large enough to accommodate the bolt [A]. Mark a point on the frame directly in line with the bolt hole and drill another hole. This is where the locking plate will be situated. Recess the locking plate into the frame and screw in place [B].

Fitting a door guard is also an easy job with no special skill required, as the components are all face fixed. Place the door guard a few inches above the door handle and position the receiving bracket on the doorframe. Mark, pilot drill [C] and screw fix. The fixing plate may have to be recessed to finish flush with the door. Position the bolt arm on the door, mark, pilot drill and screw fix [D]. Check that the alignment of the bolt arm and receiving bracket is correct [E] and then adjust as necessary.

Fitting good locks and bolts is essential. Cheap locks are a poor buy, but good locks poorly fitted are not much better

Tools Required:

Drill
Drill bits
Screwdriver
Scissors
Card

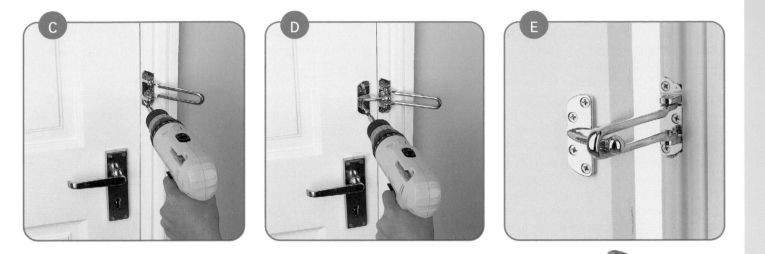

than useless. Bolts are very good for security, but are only useable when you're at home.

My bare minimum recommendations for good door security would be a deadlocking cylinder rim lock fitted about a third of the way down from the door top and a mortise lock fitted about a third up from the bottom. Personally, I would also have a second mortise lock fitted to the central door rail, lockable with matching keys to the bottom mortise lock. (The local locksmiths can match a second lock to the first.) I would also fit a third hinge centrally if the door only had two, as this will strengthen the whole door and reduce the likelihood of it being smashed or kicked in on its hinged side!

Packing out door bolts sometimes become necessary if there has been movement or expansion in the door. Unscrew and remove the catch plate on the frame [F]. Pack out with small pieces of card until you get the correct alignment of the bolt and catch plate [G]. Screw back into place.

TOMMY'S TIP

If you don't have any glass panels in your doors or the fitted glass is obscure, fit a peephole, which allows you to observe whoever is calling by means of the unique convex lens. Peepholes are inexpensive and simple to fit. Attach a security chain or door guard to prevent people from forcing their way past as you open the door. Again, these are inexpensive and easy to install.

WINDOW SECURITY

Window security: people talk about it as if it's something that has only been required since the Seventies – I do mean the 1970s. It seems that prior to that decade, in the Swinging Sixties, we didn't worry about it because we were all too busy being sexually liberated. Or was it that we didn't have much to steal? Strangely enough, and unfortunately, my memories of the Sixties are quite different. Liberation for me came about with David Bowie and Al Green in the early Seventies (musically, I mean). I'm sorry, I digress. 'Window security': the Victorians were well aware of the vulnerability of windows, so they designed various catches and window locks, but the most successful anti-burglary devices were the very aesthetically pleasing window shutters of the period. Again, the Victorians created an impressive design, for the shutters were multi-purpose. When closed, the window became almost impregnable and provided privacy and warmth, whilst allowing a certain amount of natural light through the top section of the window above the shutters. They are just as effective today. When the occupants of the house are at home and the shutters are open, they form a complimentary surround to the window, creating a pleasant focal point in the room. If you're not lucky enough to have shutters in your home, you may have to resort to using modern methods, such as purpose made window locks.

I don't approve of bars outside the window to provide security – they are dangerous barriers in the event of a fire, and they look ugly. If you feel you need a steel barrier of some sort, try the folding concertina type that are fixed internally, are far less obtrusive, but do the job.

Window security is extremely important, as this is one of the most vulnerable areas of your home, so invest in good quality locks and ensure they are well fitted.

CHANGING AN EXISTING CASEMENT FASTENER FOR A LOCKABLE HANDLE

The first thing to do is to remove the existing handle and catch. Use your screwdriver for this and take care not to slip and damage the wood. You may have to fill one or two of the holes with filler as the new handle and catch will probably not match the existing fixing holes.

Offer up the new catch to the fixed part of the window in the same location as the existing one. Using the bradawl, press into the wood, twisting as you go through the holes in the catch [A]. This will make small pilot holes for the fixing screws. Now screw the catch firmly to the window frame [B].

TOMMY'S TIP

If you are unable to afford good locks, a simple alternative is to drill through the sash into the frame or central mullion, and secure it with a thumbscrew. Alternatively, use an ordinary thick brass screw (no. 10 or 12) but ensure that you don't catch the edge of the glass pane with either the drill or screw! Also, use a drill bit that is fractionally narrower than the screw you're going to use.

Tools Required:

Screwdriver
Bradawl
Drill
Bits
Tape measure

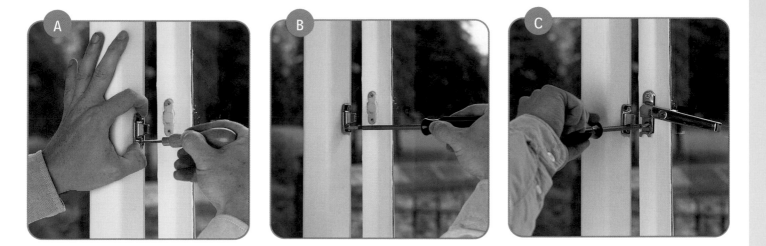

To fix the lockable handle to the opening casement side, mark your holes and place the handle over the catch. Close the window, wedging it with paper, and mark the holes. Now use the bradawl to make the pilot holes as before and finally screw the handle to the casement window [C].

FIXING A SWING LOCK

This type of lock is also an ideal replacement for a standard fastener. It's a neat, unobtrusive little lock, which is usually supplied in a white powder coated finish. The lock is fitted in exactly the same way as the lockable handle fastener; screw the plate to the window frame [D]; use a bradawl to make fixing holes for the catch on the window [E]; check alignment and screw the catch onto the window [F]. Keep the lock functioning perfectly by lubricating occasionally with light oil. Sounds a bit like my routine 'the occasional lubrication', to function perfectly....

OTHER LOCKS

There are a variety of locks available for every type and style of window – for example, dual screws for sash windows, which are inexpensive but effective. My preference is to fit sash stops, which allow the window to be left slightly open for ventilation, but remain secure. Safety wise, they score well by preventing children from opening the windows. A cockspur handle lock can be easily fitted to a wooden casement window, via a lockable extending bolt, which traps the handle. Metal casement windows, however, may be a little more difficult to attach locks to, as they may require the drilled holes to be threaded, using a die normally supplied with the locking kit. Large casements and pivot windows may require the use of rack bolts or casement locks. Alternatively fit a 'stay arm lock', which is fixed below the stay, with a lockable bolt passed through one of the stay arm holes. If this doesn't suit, change the stay arm for a purpose-made lockable type.

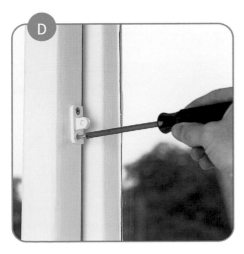

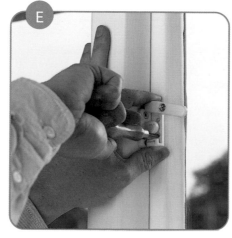

REPLACING PANES OF GLASS

I remember the very first pane of glass I replaced – again it was at my parents' house. As I sit here writing I'm looking at a scar, a war wound, that I attribute to my best mate Ronnie all those years ago. We were playing darts in my sister's bedroom in her absence. Her bedroom was at the top of the house and I needed to go to the loo, which was down a short flight of stairs, then a left hand turn and down at the end of a long corridor. It was Ronnie's turn to throw and I was so desperate to go, but I knew what a big cheat he was, so I jumped the stairs and took the hard left turn at a gravity defying tilt. But it was going into the straight, recently highly polished floor by my mum that was my undoing. Dressed only in my stockinged feet, which afforded me little or no traction, I crashed into a brick chimney breast halfway down the hallway. My right knee took the brunt of the impact with my left hand punching a pane of glass out of the bathroom

door. I remember looking down at my knee and letting out a scream like a banshee. I must have passed out, because the next thing I remember was being carried by my big Uncle Dave down to his car, to take me to hospital. Some time, though, was lost in a futile attempt to find the missing section from my knee – a large piece of flesh that had been chipped out had disappeared without trace. After a long post-mortem of the events of that day, Ronnie and I had no alternative but to conclude that the missing piece of evidence had been quickly sniffed out and consumed by our big black and white tomcat, Beauty. This was probably what has put me off cats to this day....

Well, as you can imagine, my Dad made me replace the broken pane of glass in the bathroom door as a punishment for playing darts in my sister's room and not my own. As for Ronnie, the crafty little so and so, well, he got off 'Scot-free'!

REPLACING THE GLASS FROM A BEADED WINDOW

Always don a pair of thick working gloves and protective eyewear before you proceed. Starting from the top, use a hammer and chisel to gently lever out the beads from the frame. Be sure to remove all of the glass, piece by piece, as you go around the frame [A].

When you have removed all the broken glass, clean any existing compound off the frame. Now measure the inside of the frame and have the new pane cut 3mm ($1/8$in) smaller on each dimension to allow tolerance when fitting.

Run a bead of compound around the inside of the frame to seal the glass and frame. Place the lower edge of the pane on to the

bottom rebate of the frame and press the pane into place [B]. Fix the top bead first by lightly tapping the pins into place, following up with the bottom bead, and finally the side beads [C]. You can now drive the pins home using the nail set punch. Fill and sand any holes before retouching the paintwork.

Tools Required:

Protective gloves
Safety glasses
Hammer
Chisel
Glazier's hacking knife
Pincers
Putty knife
Nail set punch

REPLACING THE GLASS
FROM A PUTTIED WINDOW

Wearing thick working gloves and protective glasses, remove the broken windowpane. You may need to use strips of sticking tape to hold any broken pieces in place [D].

TOMMY'S TIP

Always take a piece of the original glass with you to the glaziers to match the correct thickness. Also, use universal putty for fixing replacement window panes. It will require kneading before you apply it, but it is certainly the best material to use.

Using the glazier's hacking knife and hammer carefully chip away the putty from the frame [E]. Starting from the top, work each piece free as you go around, also pulling out any sprigs you come across with the pincers. Clean off all remnants of old putty and seal the frame with wood primer.

Using a palm size ball of putty, press a thin line of putty to the inside of the frames [F]. The bed for the glass to press/seal against should be about 3mm ($1/8$in) thick.

Lower the bottom edge of the glass into the rebate of the frame [G]. Press all around and secure in place using the glazing sprigs. Tap the sprigs into the frame using the edge of a chisel so they lie flat against the glass. Trim the surplus putty from the inside of the frame with the putty knife [H]. Now apply an even but thick layer of putty to the outside of the frame and with the putty knife work the putty to a smooth 45º band all around the frame, mitring the corners. Allow at least 24 hours for the putty to dry. Trim off any excess before painting the putty for a final finish.

DRAUGHTPROOFING WINDOWS AND DOORS

'Wind' can cause all sorts of problems. It can make your windows and doors rattle and lower the temperature sufficiently enough to force the boiler to blast away continuously, pushing up your heating bills dramatically. The only room in a house I don't mind being cold is the bedroom. I particularly like a cold bed, with crisp white cotton sheets.

I deliberately go to bed at least 15 minutes after my wife, pausing to empty the bins outside in my bare feet, so getting my size 12s really cold before climbing into bed and planting them on my wife's (by now) roasting hot legs. One learns on these occasions that the speed and agility of a 100-metre hurdler are pre-requisites, in order to avoid the flailing fists and rapier tongue of your partner. After exiting and waiting craftily in the bathroom until the eruption subsides, and she once again falls into a peaceful slumber, I then slip back into bed and repeat the torture! If nothing else, it quite often makes for a great cure for headaches (hers, if you know what I mean!).

I was sure as a youngster that I was being groomed to work in Santa's grotto up there in Lapland. Because what I don't like are cold bathrooms. As a child growing up at home, I have to say that I think we had the coldest bathroom this side of Lapland. Our bathroom had a flat, un-insulated roof, a metal casement window, three outside solid walls, fully tiled with a linoleum floor. The bathroom was not a place for dalliance. So all six of us were the quickest bathed kids in the street. Of course, I am talking about a period before central heating was commonplace, although it wasn't actually that long ago!

As I discovered on various refurbishments of my parents' house over many years, the biggest problem by far was heat retention. Our house had the thermal qualities of an iceberg caused by a number of factors – the main one being a lack of draughtproofing of doors and windows. Efficient, good quality draughtproofing for your house will probably pay for itself in fuel savings in the first year, and sure beats serving an apprenticeship for Lapland to boot!

WINDOWS

Most hinged casement windows made of wood will at some time warp and become ill-fitting, causing draughts and a literal pain in the neck. This can easily be eliminated using a soft plastic, self-adhesive moulded draught excluder.

The draught excluder usually comes in a double width roll, which you will need to split into two single strips for windows [A]. Make sure the surfaces are clean. Starting at one end, peel off the backing paper of the strip to reveal the adhesive side [B]. This will be stuck to the outside of the fixed window frames, which the opening casement will press against when closed.

Working from the top of the right hand corner, carefully press the end of the excluder into place, leaving a 25mm (1in) trimming edge [C]. Work anti-clockwise around the edge of the frame. Cut the ends of each length at a 45° angle to form a neat joint at each corner. Close the window and secure it firmly in place to enable the excluder to stick properly.

Tools Required:

Small screwdriver
Bradawl
Scissors
Saw (optional)

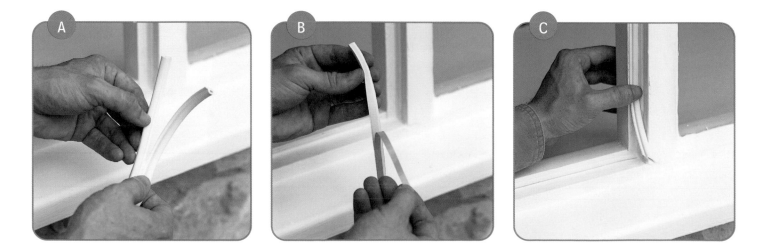

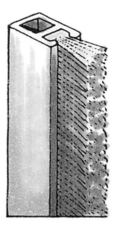

The top and bottom closing rails of a sash window can be sealed with any form of compressible excluder. The sliding edges admit fewer draughts, but they can be sealed with a brush seal fixed to the frame — inside for the lower sash, outside for the top one.

DOORS

Doorframes can be draughtproofed using the double draught excluder applied as described above. Another source of draughts in doors is the keyhole. This can be overcome by fixing what is known as an escutcheon cover plate over the keyhole [D]. Another place vulnerable to draughts is the front door letterbox opening.

You can purchase ready-made brush draught excluders, but be sure to have the dimensions of your letterbox with you when you go shopping. A little oversize is all right, but undersize is no good at all. Before you begin, remove the inside flap of the letterbox if you have one, as the brush excluder will be replacing this.

Place the brush frame over the letterbox, opening on the inside of the door. Make sure the frame is squarely over the opening, mark the holes with the bradawl and then screw the draught excluder securely to the door [E].

It really is worthwhile spending some time and money draughtproofing your home properly. You might not give this matter much thought during a warm summer (some hope!), but you wait until the autumn and winter nights close in and the wind gets up.... That's when you realize that there is no substitute for nice cosy, draught-proof windows and doors!

TOMMY'S TIP

When fitting a brush strip to the base of a door, make sure it aligns with the floor rather than the door. That way you can be sure of completely blocking the draught.

PAINTING AND VARNISHING WINDOWS AND DOORS

You often hear people say that they hate painting. Personally, I have to say that I find it very therapeutic, and when you have put a lot of effort into the preparation, the finished job is a pleasure to look at.

There are a few simple rules to creating a sound paint job on woodwork. The first and most important one is to take your time with the preparation – the old adage 'the finish is only as good as the preparation' is very, very true! Call me old fashioned, but I don't think you can beat an oil-based paint for a really wonderful finish. If you are painting new or recently fitted windows and doors, it's perfectly all right to use full gloss finish. If, however, the woodwork is much older, and may have suffered a degree of distress (a bit like me!), it may be more appropriate to use an eggshell finish, which is a semi-flat finish. This finish doesn't reflect the imperfections acquired over a period of time and gives a much classier, understated finish. For a really fine finish, I would suggest two undercoats and one topcoat, use flour paper (fine sand paper) for sanding between each coat.

People believe the myth that to obtain the best finish you have to strip every bit of old paint off, back to the original wood! Untrue. If the paint hasn't cracked, split and curled, and you don't want to wax or varnish the original wood, then providing the body of paintwork is sound, just give the surface a good sanding before repainting. This actually protects the wood better. Remember to wear a mask, as a lot of old paint contains high levels of lead. If just the sill or section of a door or window's paintwork has cracked and split, just strip the local damaged sections back to the wood. Using an electric sander or block and paper, sand down any paint edges after burning off, and paint with primer any new or unpainted surfaces before proceeding with two undercoats and one topcoat. When using a blowtorch or heat gun, proceed with care; wear all the safety equipment – goggles, gloves and mask. Do NOT use heat close to glass, as it will expand and crack. Instead, use chemical paint stripper on these areas, such as glazing bars, if it becomes necessary to strip the paint off.

VARNISHING

There are many different types of wood varnish, but all need to be applied in the same fashion to achieve that perfect finish.

Your door or window will need to be prepared as you would for painting. If you have bare wood, this should be brushed free of any particles.

Thin the first coat by 10 per cent to form a sealer coat. Apply the sealer using a brush [A]. Always apply varnish in the direction of the wood grain and allow enough time inbetween coats for the varnish to dry in accordance with the manufacturer's instructions.

Lightly key the surface with the fine flour sandpaper in between coats [B] and then, using a cloth and white spirit, clean the surface and apply a full coat of varnish. Apply a third coat for that really perfect finish.

PAINTING DOORS

Preparation is all-important when painting doors. Remove all the door furniture (and keep the handle in the room with you, just in case). If painting on bare wood, any knots should be treated with knot solution and the door primed. If you are painting the door different colours inside and out, paint the

Tools Required:

Brushes – medium, fine
Flour sandpaper
White spirit
Cloth
Window scraper
Paint stripper
Mask
Safety glasses
Protective gloves

outer edge of the door the same colour as the inside opening face, with each frame matching the closing face of the door. If you are painting a flush door, start at the top and use a mini roller, working down in vertical sections blending one into the other [C]. Lay on the paint, then finish each vertical section with light strokes. Finally, paint the edges using a 25mm (1in) brush to avoid any paint seams [D].

PAINTING WINDOWS

When painting windows, you will first need to remove the levers, catches and stays and then keep the window open using some stiff wire looped around a nail driven into the underside of the open casement and hooked into one of the screw holes on the frame. Clean the glass before painting the window.

Prepare the surface by sanding and wipe away any residue. Paint the outside of the casement first, always starting on the innermost edge and moving to the outer surfaces. Follow up by painting the fixed window frame from the beading or putty surface, then moving to the face of the frame. You can either mask the edge of

your windows with masking tape to avoid getting paint on the windows, or remove any overspill with a window scraper afterwards. Remember, for all painting, use the first third of the brush. Do not overload the brush with paint [E].

Always clean paint brushes with white spirit for oil-based paints, followed by soap and water. Dry the brushes in some kitchen roll and wrap the bristles in newspaper, folding it to the shape of the brush and securing it around the handle with an elastic band. Follow this advice and the next time you use your brush it will be as good as new. You'll also save a fortune not having to buy new brushes for every job!

TOMMY'S TIP

If you have the time and want the perfect paint finish, take the door off and lay it flat on stools or a bench. Prepare the door all round properly, clean off residue with a cloth and white spirit, and then apply your paint or varnish as described. Leave it to dry thoroughly before turning the door over and painting the other side!

When painting over putty, first ensure the putty has a hard skin to paint over, and secondly make sure that the paint covers all the putty and a fraction of the glass to create a waterproof seal.

INSTALLING EXTERNAL SECURITY LIGHTING

Security lighting covers a wide range of different products, and with some simple but clever designing these lighting systems can be effective but unobtrusive. Your selection also depends very much on how you want your lighting to work. It may be practical to have some low voltage background lighting, or you may think that high-powered sensor floodlights are appropriate. However, beware, as some people say these lights are an invasion of privacy! This reminds me of a story about somebody who shall remain anonymous – let's call him Robert. Robert has a row with his partner. He ends up sleeping on the sofa. He awakes early and leaves for work before his partner arises. Robert's got the hump all day, and decides to go for a drink with the boys after work. The crack is good and soon Robert thinks, 'Well, I might as well get hung for a sheep as a lamb!', and decides on a couple more. Well, the evening disappears as fast as his sobriety, until he discovers he's either lost his keys, or they are at home, which means waking up his partner. Not such a good idea! Thinking desperately hard, he has a drink-induced brainstorm. 'I'll climb over the back fence, get the spare key to the back door under the flowerpot, and sneak up to bed.' He

eventually manages to drag himself over the fence, rolls and crashes straight into a shrubbery. This proves extremely painful, but having semi-successfully completed the first stage of his plan, he decides to answer a strong call of nature. He chooses to relieve himself in the garden, so as not to alert his partner indoors. As he shuffles around, suddenly it seems that daylight has arrived. The light is so bright he can't see anything and is frozen to the spot. At this point, his partner and her parents (who have been invited over for their anniversary dinner, which he's obviously forgotten), peer out of the upstairs window to see what has caused the security floodlights to come on, just catching sight of an intruder scurrying into the shadows. Robert's partner's father is very sporty. A rugby coach and judo instructor, he runs downstairs into the garden to tackle this intruder (who hasn't finished peeing yet), with a flying tackle at groin height. The result is very messy, as the tackle catapults Robert and his father-in-law into the large koi carp pond. After a short struggle, the police arrive. They eventually sort everything out, although Robert's state of undress is hotly debated by the police, who wonder whether he could be charged as a flasher!

MAINS OPERATED SYSTEMS

There are two main popular systems of security lighting – dusk-to-dawn lighting, which works automatically when triggered by the ambient light levels, or the passive infra-red sensor system, which will only come on if something crosses the remote detector, therefore avoiding unnecessary wastage of electricity.

To fit these lights is pretty simple, by either linking into the existing lighting circuit, or via a 13-amp plug to an electrical socket. All lights are normally supplied with

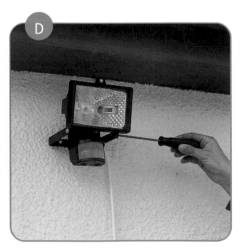

BATTERY OPERATED SENSOR LIGHTS

Sensor light systems that are purely battery powered are not readily available as an off-the-shelf stock item. However, specialist electrical retailers and wholesalers can obtain kits by special order.

instructions, which you should always read thoroughly before beginning work.

Unscrew the rear light cover to reveal the connection terminals [A], attach the flex [B] and secure the rear cover. After selecting the light position carefully, firstly secure the mounting brackets to the wall, by hammer drilling, and fixing with plugs and screws [C], which are normally provided with the security light. Carefully attach the light unit to the bracket [D], ensuring that you do not touch the lamp inside. Next, simply roll out and secure the flex to the wall, or the weather-boarding beneath the eaves of the house, as shown in our illustrated example [E]. Alternatively, drill a hole through the wall directly behind the lamp and feed the cable directly inside.

This is where you decide to connect the light to the house electrical supply, or simply connect to a 13-amp plug into a socket [F]. For safety reasons, I recommend the use of an RCD when connecting any outside electrical appliance into the domestic power supply. You may have to adjust the pre-set timer of the security light to suit your personal requirements [G].

Individual sensors can be prepared and installed independently of the light fitting, to enlarge the catchment area or to create an early warning system [H].

TOMMY'S TIP

Don't fit a security light if you're regularly late home from the pub!

Tools Required:

Hammer drill
Electrical screwdriver
Wire strippers
Hammer
Screwdriver

INSTALLING AN EXTERNAL POWER SOURCE

It's shocking the amount of people who use electrical equipment outside without taking the correct safety precautions. Basically, you should always use an RCD (residual current device). Let me explain. When using electrical appliances and tools outside, it's likely the conditions may be damp and users are likely to be in direct contact with the earth, which may easily result in fatal accidents if strict safety procedures are not adhered to. An RCD cuts off the power in a fraction of a second before the tool user can receive an electric shock. Adaptor RCDs are the simplest type to use. They just plug into any socket outlet, and you can then plug your lead or appliance into the RCD. As an added precaution, wear thick rubber-soled footwear.

I treat electricity with the greatest of respect, having had a few close calls myself. Talking of thick soled boots reminds me of my teenage school days when stacks were in fashion, and I used to be the roadie for a school rock band. They were called the 'Madison Blues Band', and they were pretty 'wicked', but the big problem was, they didn't have anywhere to practise. Well, my Dad was a very tolerant man, so he allowed the group to practise at the yard. While the slab making was taking place on one side of the yard, we had 'Woodstock' going on at the other. It really was a peculiar sight, with a small audience gathering at tea break to watch these kids with long hair and strange clothes make weird loud music in the open air. It really was fantastic. We even managed to get some of the old timers' foot tapping, but the one complaint we had was that it was too loud. Our yard was in Barking, Essex and we could be heard about 5 miles away down the A13 in Rainham. We had a huge amount of equipment, which we plugged directly into the commercial supply – this was before the days of the residual circuit devices, and I remember a truck driving over the extension lead and cutting it. There was water around from the paving production and I remember getting an almighty wallop from the power. We were lucky nobody was badly injured or killed. Sadly, Dad stopped the music sessions after that; he thought it was too dangerous for us. Now fortunately we have RCDs, which from a safety point of view, is definitely music to my ears!

TOMMY'S TIP

If you think fitting an external socket, like this one, is too difficult a job for you, then fit RCD plugs to your extension leads to ensure the safety of your family and friends. But make sure that the RCD isn't removed from the socket.

A wide range of outdoor power sockets are available for sale – the type demonstrated here is good quality and water-resistant with a built in RCD (residual current device). The ideal situation would be to run 2.5mm twin and earth cable from the external socket through the wall to the consumer unit. Alternatively, you could add to the existing power ring main, or simply add a spur from an existing socket to provide the power source.

Drill through the wall with a suitable masonry bit and hammer drill. Feed through the 2.5mm twin and earth cable. N.B. DO NOT CONNECT TO THE RING MAIN UNTIL AFTER

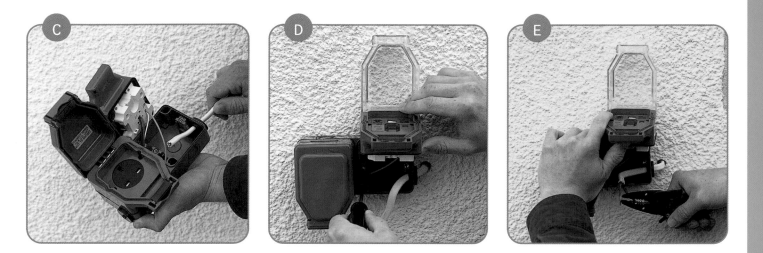

COMPLETING THE FITTING OF THE EXTERNAL SOCKET!
Unscrew the switch face and lift out [A] to reveal the cable connection terminals [B]. Feed the cable through the protective rubber flange [C]. Position the socket in place, and mark the fixing points. Using a masonry drill to create the holes, fix the socket with plugs and screws [D].

Use cable strippers to reveal the wire conductors [E] and connect the conductors to the appropriate terminals: red = live; black = neutral; yellow and green = earth [F].

Screw back the socket face [G], and make the internal connections to the power supply (as covered in Changing Sockets, pp 24–5). Finally, switch on the power supply, plug in the lawnmower [H], close the cover [I] and proceed happily with your SAFE mowing.

Tools Required:

Masonry drill and bits
Hammer
Electrical screwdriver
Screwdriver
or cordless driver
Cable stripper

INSTALLING AN EXTERNAL WATER TAP

A water tap in the wrong place can be a blooming nightmare! That's why I can't understand people who don't fit an outside tap for the garden. Let me ask you a question – have you every tried fitting a hose to a kitchen mixer tap? You can do it with a special kit, but it's still nigh on impossible! You know the very worst thing that occurs with these or any other indoor tap attachment? When you come back indoors from the garden after merrily watering your plants, it looks like an episode of 'London's Burning' has been shot in your house, and at least 20 firemen have emptied the local reservoir into your kitchen!

Do I sound like I speak from experience? Oh yes! There was one particular time when a tap in the wrong place gave me a terrible fright, and a whack around the ear to boot.

My Dad's building block manufacturing plant was a small family-type affair. My Dad's Mum, my Gran, used to attend work on a Saturday, cleaning up and cooking for everyone. We had a lovely old cast iron pot-bellied stove for heating. There was also an old butler sink but the tap had to be turned on and off from the room next door. One of my jobs was to light the

pot-bellied stove for Gran, and at times it was really difficult to light. The truth is I was a touch impetuous in those days, and had what I thought was a brilliant idea. I took a three-quarters empty can of paint thinners from the stores and, after lighting the fire in the stove, attempted to pour on the thinners to speed the process along. The result was a terrifying shock, because the fire blew back into the can and exploded the volatile gases. The whole room was on fire in several different places. I tried beating out the flames with a towel, which only served to spread the flames even more. I then had to run next door to turn the tap on and run back. I tipped the bowl full of cups and plates out into the butler sink, breaking most of them, then throwing bowls of water around the room onto the flames to extinguish them. I did succeed, but it was one of the most frightening moments of my life, and to cap it all off, Gran was whacking me around the head for breaking all her crockery. I also thought my Dad was going to kill me.

This story emphasizes how important it is to have a tap in the right place. I'm not saying it would have prevented the fire, but I might have avoided the wrath of Gran!

Conventional ways of fitting an external tap usually consist of installing a 'Tee joint' in the mains supply, and running a copper pipe through the wall to an external tap known as a 'bibcock'. There are various different ways of installing an external water tap, especially since the introduction of plastic water pipes. Here, I show just one way of installing an outside tap quickly and simply.

The first step is to fit a connection to the existing cold feed line on the non-pressure side of the stop valve. You can do this by fitting a self-bore valve. This will make a hole in the pipe without you having to turn off the water if necessary.

Place the saddle over the pipe and screw this onto the back plate. This will firmly fix it over the pipe ready for the valve [A].

Now slowly but firmly screw in the valve [B], making sure beforehand that it's in the OFF position. Insert the valve until you are sure you have made a hole in the pipe, keeping the valve in the vertical position with the outlet down. Using an adjustable spanner, tighten up the lock nut on the valve onto the saddle to secure a watertight joint [C]. Now screw on the hose to the valve outlet [D].

Using your hammer drill and bit, drill a hole in the external wall from the inside out, checking its location both inside and

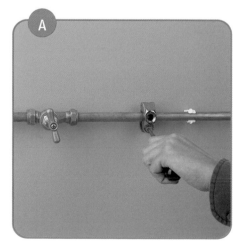

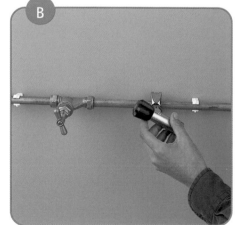

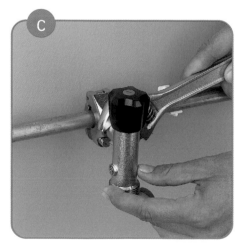

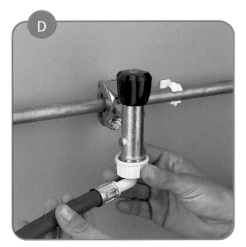

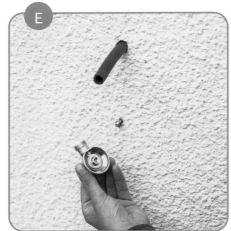

out to make sure it arrives where you want it. It wouldn't do to have the hole appearing behind the roof drainage down pipe, would it? Now pass the flexible hose through the wall [E]. Next, you will need to fix the tap back plate onto the wall, vertically in line with the hose about 150–200mm (6–8in) below the hole. Having drilled a hole for the back plate screw, fix your screw to the wall using a wall plug of a suitable size and then screw the tap back plate to this. Install the tap in a vertical position with the inlet for the hose connector pointing up. Fit a jubilee clip over the hose and the hose over the male side of the connector. Tighten the jubilee clip for a watertight connection [F], but not so tight as to cut into the hose. Now screw the female connector onto the male tap connector and tighten finger tight [G]. Finally, screw on the body of the tap [H].

Each winter, remember to isolate the outside tap against freezing by turning the inside tap to the OFF position and the outside tap to the ON position, to drain off any residue.

TOMMY'S TIP

Buy the right attachments. I don't wish to sound patronizing, but plan carefully what you want, ensuring that you have the correct materials and tools to do the job. (And have the phone number of a local plumber handy – just in case!)

Tools Required:

Adjustable spanner
Hammer drill
Masonry bit
Screwdriver
Rawl plugs

PATIO REPAIRS

I was regularly taken to work by my Dad from the age of four. The idea behind this was to keep me out of mischief, but he didn't reckon on the outcome: as a result of those early experiences at the block-making plant, I have made, handled and laid more paving than I care to remember!

What I do find surprising though is that people are prepared to pay thousands to a contractor to landscape their garden, and then just leave it. Imagine what your car would be like if you never serviced it. Would you remember what colour or make it was if you didn't clean it for a couple of years? But people do exactly that to their gardens. I had better point out that I'm referring to the hard landscaping parts of people's gardens. Maybe that's why it happens. People think because it's hard, it doesn't require any TLC. Well it does! TLC is not the exclusive domain of horticulturalists – in actual fact I'm thinking of starting 'Tommy's Exemplary Slabbers' Tender Loving Care Loyal Enthusiasts Society', or 'TESTLCLES' for short.

Problems naturally occur on patios if you have a north-facing garden; algae and lichen flourish in the damp conditions of these gardens, so if you really want to revive your patio to its former glory, here are a few pointers.

Paving slabs should be laid on a mortar bed, NOT sand. If they are, pick them up, clean them off and relay the slabs on a mortar bed. Do not 'spot' the mortar, or you'll be overrun with insects. Lay the slabs on a full mortar bed (which Alan Titchmarsh calls 'Tommy's magic mortar') for paving – four parts sharp sand, two parts soft sand, one part cement. Use a bucket to gauge the materials accurately. Make the mix wet by adding water and keep it pliable by adding plasticizer to the mix.

If your patio has been well-laid but has become dirty, or algae covered, remove the algae by using an acid patio cleaner. There are various good proprietary brands. Follow the instructions carefully, and remember that goggles, gloves and wellies are required. Mix the chemical with water and apply with a watering can [A], vigorously rub over the surface with a yard broom and rinse with cold water, for a surface almost as good as new!

Weeds and debris will not grow if the paving is laid on a full mortar bed and grouted. However, if your patio has been laid on sand and you do have this problem, rake out the weeds and debris using a trowel and chisel [B], sweep off and re-point the gaps between the slabs. Re-pointing, using 'Tommy's

Tools Required:

Club hammer
Small bolster chisel
Cold chisel
Shovel
Yard broom
Soft brush
Watering can
Mixing board/mixer
Trowel
Jointer

magic grouting mixture' is three parts DRY soft sand to one part cement. Sweep this into the joints [C], forcing home with a gloved hand, and then rub over the joints with a jointer.

To replace a damaged slab, first rake out the jointing surrounding the slab using a cold chisel and club hammer [D], break out the damaged slab with a crowbar, levering it against an offcut of wood to prevent damage to the neighbouring slab [E] and then re-bed the replacement slab [F]. You can use dry mortar sprinkled into the hole, then wet it down with a watering can before the slab is laid, although my personal preference is to use wet mortar.

Ensure that the replacement slab is level with the surrounding paving, by tapping down to match perfectly all round. Use a rubber mallet, or the handle of a club hammer to gently tap the slab into place [G]. All that's left to do now is the pointing, by using the same method I mentioned earlier [H].

TOMMY'S TIP

Check each slab for its face side before laying it, so that all the slabs are laid best side up. Also, lay the slab immediately after setting down the wet mortar. Otherwise the mortar will dry out quickly, and trying to force the slab down may result in the new slab breaking.

REPAIRING A FENCE

I always advise people to discuss the plans they have for their fences with their neighbours. Even though you may own the fence, what you choose to do or 'not do' will have some effect on their lives, because they will have to look at it. If you want to replace a 0.75m (2ft 6in) open picket fence with a 2m (6ft 6in) close boarded or panelled fence, your neighbours may well feel offended – and rightly so, because the lack of light will affect their garden as well as yours! A compromise may be to have the first section at 1.8m (6ft) high for privacy, where you possibly may eat, drink and entertain, and the rest of the garden at a much more civilized 1m (3ft). My tip, though, is whatever you decide upon, chat to your neighbours about it before actually erecting it.

'Not a lot of people know that' (I'm beginning to sound like Michael Caine...!), you are supposed to show the best side of your fence towards your neighbour, as a sign of common courtesy. Likewise, your other neighbour should show the best side of their fence towards you, and so on and so on. The normal rule of thumb is that if the posts are on your side of the fence, then that fence is yours. When the posts are between the panels, who owns what becomes less clear. If uncertain, check the deeds, or consult your solicitor to ensure that the fence you are repairing or replacing is in fact yours!

At work, I have had some extremely difficult neighbours in the past, not least that neighbour on television who didn't want a shed erected anywhere near his fence, even though it wasn't even in his garden. Then there was the fence I had to erect for friends of mine, Tommy and Sally, at 'war with next door', so they didn't consult their neighbours and I had to fit a complete boundary fence without stepping onto the neighbour's property – which I can tell you, is not easy. I have even had to take down a completed fence for the sake of 50mm (2in) out of alignment at one end, covering a huge area of land. All these problems can be avoided by a little consultation with the neighbours. Fences really can cause emotions to boil over. Another problem which can cause great antagonism is the indifferent neighbour who is totally unconcerned by their own dilapidated fence. So to all you apathetic fence owners out there, be kind and neighbourly: fix up that broken fence and put a smile back on your neighbour's face.

TOMMY'S TIP

To remove the remains of an old post, dig a hole alongside it and lever the old remains into the new hole. Once freed, it simply lifts out. Use a good wood preservative to protect the bottom of your new post before setting it into the vacated hole.

There are basically two types of common fence. The first is the gravel board variety (named after the bit of the fence in contact with the soil), which doesn't rot and is used in conjunction with concrete posts and wooden panels. Although maintenance-free, this type of fence doesn't exactly blend into the background. The second common type of fence is made completely of wood – preferably pressure-treated. When the bottom gravel board panels rot, they can be simply replaced with a new piece by means of a couple of screws at either end into the base of the post [A].

Most timber fencing products arrive in a very uninspiring mud brown, or soon-to-fade golden brown, water-based dip

Tools Required:

Cordless drill
Spirit level
String line
Shovel
Long bar
Hole borer
Hammer
Sledgehammer

solution. I would recommend that you apply your own preservative coating, either water- or spirit-based, available in a fantastic range of colours, but as you can see from the picture, I've been working with Alan far too long. He's got me painting everything blue now [B]. Where is the 'phone number of that psychiatrist!

Erecting a new post is simple once you have removed the remains of the old one. The new post needs a hole a minimum depth of 460mm (18in) to hold. Use a stiff concrete mix dry or

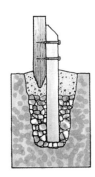

If the base of your wooden post rots underground, you can make a passable repair by bracing the upper section with a short concrete spur. In fact, this is my preferred option for fixing new wooden posts as well as for making repairs.

with not too much water – it should be the consistency of double cream. Pack the concrete in around the post with a wooden batten [C].

Ensure the post is level on two adjoining sides, and aligned with the other posts by use of a string line. Attach some temporary braces to keep the post upright whilst the concrete sets [D].

Obviously, softwood posts only last so long in the soil. To increase the post life, use pressure-treated posts. Alternatively stand the posts upright in a bucket of preservative for a minimum of two days, to help extend the lifespan of the post [E].

Popular today, and to avoid digging, are the use of metpost spikes. I have mixed feelings about them, but they can be a useful alternative to concreting. You must knock them in straight, using the resin block supplied, with the sweet swing of a sledgehammer [F]. Once the metpost is firmly in the ground, simply slip the end of your post into it [G].

Repairing a Fence

REPAIRING/ REALIGNING A GATE

First impressions – that's what a gate gives any visitor to your home, but maybe more importantly, what does it say to a potential buyer? In fact, the front gate is the very first thing a visitor to your house touches!

If the front gate is falling apart, that sends out a certain message. If the gate doesn't fit properly, that sends out a different message. And if the gate has paint peeling off, that won't encourage the visitor or potential buyer that they're necessarily going to enjoy the visit. This may all sound a bit OTT, but seriously, just close your eyes and visualize a pretty cottage. I bet it has a perfectly painted front gate – not one that's hanging off, with hardly any paint left on it! So, make a lovely job of the front gate and hope nobody notices that Handy Andy has been working on the rest of the house! (Now Andy, don't get upset, you know I'm only joking!) Take note that if you make a beautiful job of your front gate,

ensure the gate is securely fixed, or your wonderful front gate could end up making an appearance at somebody else's dream cottage.

When I bought my house, there were only a couple of rotten pieces of the front gate remaining – in actual fact, a bit like the rest of the house. The gate was the original – 55 years old – so I couldn't complain. My neighbour also still has his house's original gate, but he maintains it regularly, and I think it will last another 55 years (at least). The gate was originally made from English oak, so I made a replacement in English oak using the original furniture. However, I didn't allow for the damp winter, and the gate expanded between the two piers, which forced it to go bow-shaped. Of course, you accept the plaudits wherever you can – people actually think it's a contemporary version of the original design! (Absolutely, darling!)

TOMMY'S TIP

Check that your gate post is in absolutely perfect alignment before attempting to hang a new gate. Also, try not to use traditional paint finishes on gates or fences. You will make a better job using wood preservative, available in a large array of colours. This will protect the wood, making it less prone to rot.

Ageing gates are a bit like us – as they get older, they start sagging and generally start heading south, no longer aligning with the gate catch on the post. To re-align the catch, use a drill to create pilot holes for re-fixing [A]. If only it were that easy to realign all our own sagging parts!

Timber shrinks as it dries out, so a good tip is to use slightly longer screws to create a firm fixing [B]. If the gate has a rotten section or two, lay the gate on a pair of stools or a work bench before working on it. Carefully remove the offending rotten pieces, using a claw hammer, pinchers, a screwdriver or whichever tool seems the most appropriate [C].

Using an existing section of the gate as a template, cut and shape a replacement piece of new timber [D]. Ensure that the replacement timber has a good few coats of preservative [E],

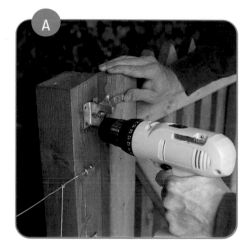

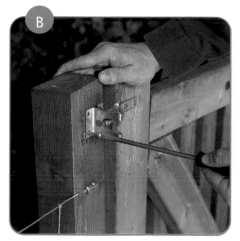

128

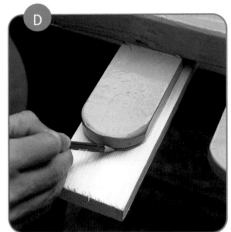

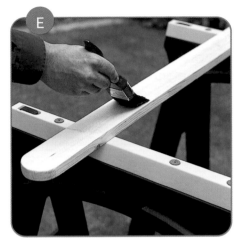

and two as an absolute minimum, before fixing the new section to the gate.

Pilot drill and countersink the fixing screws for the new picket or replacement section [F]. Fill over the screw heads, sandpaper the whole gate down thoroughly and re-coat it with preservative, not forgetting to paint the gate posts as well.

If you choose paint instead of wood preservative for your gate, be warned that it will not protect the gate as thoroughly and this means that the life of your gate is likely to be foreshortened by rot or blistering. Before painting, ensure that any bare wood is properly primed, and then apply a minimum of two undercoats and one topcoat. When you are satisfied, re-hang the gate [G], ensuring that it clears the path and aligns perfectly with its posts.

Now stand back, open your eyes and see if it matches the gate in your dream about an idyllic country cottage!

If you are setting new gateposts into concrete, attach battens to them to support them as the concrete sets. Use a spirit level to ensure that the posts are absolutely upright before you attach the battens.

Tools Required:

Cordless drill
Screwdriver
Saw
Jigsaw
Claw hammer
Pinchers
Paintbrush
Sandpaper

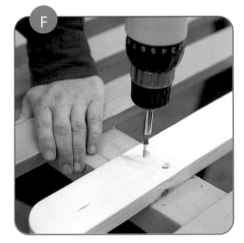

MAKING AND ERECTING TRELLIS

I really like trellis – its uses are many and very flexible, so it continues to increase in popularity. The introduction of tanalized softwood (that is, pressure-treated) has enabled us to create all manner of expensive-looking constructions for a fraction of the cost of using hardwood.

I'm a great supporter of using treated softwood, because properly managed softwood forests replace two trees for every one felled (which is certainly the case in Europe now), so it's a terrific renewable material source. All it needs to grow is sun and rain, and there is very little damage to the ozone layer through the creation of this product.

There is something extremely pleasing about making these panels and structures yourself. The most satisfying for me to date were those in the garden constructed in the memory of the lovely Jill Dando. I designed and constructed four large pergola arches, purpose-made with built-in trellis panels to complete the perfect piece. I owe great thanks to my mate 'Jimmy the Joiner' and his wife Rosemary, who machined all the components for me, and then came down to give Willie and me a hand to put it all together. What a task we faced with the painting of the arches. There were over a thousand components which all had to be coated in – guess what colour? Yes, it was BLUE. Although Alan chose the colour, it was aptly named 'Forget-me-not Blue' – very appropriate, I thought. Luckily we had lots of volunteers to help us with the painting, which is normally carried out by Charlie and members of the crew. (I wouldn't mind painting, honest! But I'm normally busy building! Shame, that!)

In years gone by, we were forced to accept poor quality and unimaginative products, and trellis was a typical example. It was only available in standard size panels of 6ft x 1, 2, 3, 4, 5 and 6ft, in dipped softwood in a range of one colour – brown. Thankfully that is no longer the case. With a little bench top table saw, DIY-ers can cut and shape the designs very much the way they want from pressure-treated softwood, painted in the colour of their choice.

Tools Required:

Saw
Jigsaw
Hammer
Spirit level
Adjustable square
Tape measure
Cordless drill
Masonry drill
Screwdriver
Paintbrush

People often want to increase the height of an existing boundary. A simple and attractive method of achieving this without breaking the bank is to add a trellis.

To fix a post to a wall, first using a sharp saw, cut the post to half its width – a minimum distance of 610mm (2ft) up from the bottom. After treating the exposed cut surface with preservative [A], attach it to the wall with frame fixings or plugs and screws [B]. Run a string line to align all the posts, using thin packers to adjust the posts to suit the spirit level and string line. Simply pilot drill and screw fix the trellis panels to the posts [C]. Purchase – or make and fix – flat post caps, to protect the post end grain from the weather.

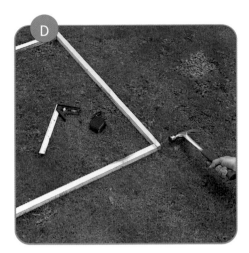

I like to make the trellis panels myself. A really simple trellis to make is the diamond pattern – which doesn't half look good!

Once the panel size has been decided (remember, you are no longer restricted to standard size panels), make an outside frame and just nail the components together using ring nails [D]. These nails have a type of thread which prevents the panel from parting.

Set your 45° angle with the adjustable square, mark the frame and nail on the first batten. Using equal spacers top and bottom, set out and fix the next batten [E]. Repeat this process across the frame. Again using the adjustable square, reverse the pattern using the same spacers, fixing the battens across the first layer of battens, once again fix by using ring nails. All that's left to do now is trim off the excess timber to form the perfect panel [G]. Finally, choose your colour (blue, if you must!).

To make a square trellis, the process is the same as above but using the spacers at a 90° angle to each layer [H]. Remember that the length of the spacers determines the size of the holes.

TOMMY'S TIP

Roofing batten is perfect for making trellis panels, because it is cheap to buy and is pressure-treated. Roofing batten is sold in two width sizes – the smaller tile batten, or the larger slate batten. I always buy the slate batten, and then run it through the saw right down the middle, thus doubling the quantity of material. A local joiner might cut it down for you, if you ask nicely....

Making and Erecting Trellis

BUILDING A BARBECUE

There is nothing better than outdoor cooking, but a word of caution – at our house, we always pre-cook our meat before we barbecue, to avoid any possibility of food poisoning. Our barbecue is a small portable type, a bit like our present garden, which is too small for a brick barbecue. Most people would like to have a permanent barbecue, but contrary to popular opinion, a brick-built barbecue is not cheap! Depending on the quality of the bricks you choose, with the grill kit, the cost would be somewhere in the region of £150–200, and then of course you have to build it yourself. Next, you need to be extremely careful where you position the barbecue. Not too close to the house, or all the cooking smells blow back indoors, to say nothing of the smoke. Barbecues should be kept separate from the main patio area, because as the cooking takes place, fat unavoidably spits out from the food and stains the paving, which is almost impossible to

remove. Don't build the barbecue too near a tree or a fence because you will create a fire hazard. (A friend of mine set fire to his fence and pergola!) As the outdoor chef in our household, I find the main problem with brick-built barbecues is that I'm normally facing in the opposite direction to everyone else – detached, as it were, from all the fun! You have to concentrate on the job in hand to avoid burnt offerings, plus if you're in shorts, look after anything else that might receive a 'right roasting'!

All this may suggest that I am against brick-built barbecues – I'm not. I have built many over the years, but unfortunately people don't often listen to the voice of experience mainly because it doesn't fit in with their plans. This is where problems result. I have a portable barbecue, so that I can pack it away when I don't need it, particularly in winter.

However, if you have the space, the time, and it is positioned appropriately, a brick-built barbecue is great!

The site chosen for this barbecue was a paved utility area, to the side of the main patio. The garden was large, so the barbecue didn't suddenly become the dominant feature. Wherever you decide to build your barbecue, it must be on a solid hardstand (a bit of concrete or paving).

Make a wooden frame to act as a template guide to the dimensions of the grill kit. Lay the bricks out dry (without mortar) to enable the correct brickwork bond to be determined. Bed the bricks on a bed of mortar made up of five parts soft building sand to one part cement, with plasticizer added [A].

Use a spirit level to ensure the brickwork is level and plumb. Here, I'm using a paving slab to act as a tabletop. Lay the slab down as a guide to the independent leg position [B]. I usually use a 1 x 0.6m (3 x 2ft) paving slab, but a 0.6 x 0.6m (2 x 2ft) like this one will suffice.

To get the brickwork bond correct, it's necessary to cut half bricks. Cut these on a soft surface with a bolster chisel and club hammer [C]. Don't forget your gloves and goggles.

Tools Required:

Spirit level
Trowel
Club hammer
Bolster chisel
Jointer
Safety glasses
Protective gloves

When you've built the brickwork to the correct height for the slab table, turn some of the bricks as shown [D], so that they act as corbels (supports) for the table and the grate.

The corbels are repeated again two courses up to support the cooking griddle [E]. Two more courses of bricks are required to complete the barbecue. Push four metal pins into the mortar below the top course of brickwork to support the warming griddle shelf [F]. I sometimes fit a flat coping or brick-on-edge course to finish off. More importantly, it's somewhere to rest my beer while I'm cooking!

Bed the paving slab on mortar to make your table top [G]. Leave the brickwork to cure for a couple of hours. Then, using a jointer (bent copper pipe or garden hose will suffice), rake out the mortar, to make a tidy job. Finally, take a soft hand brush and carefully brush over the brickwork to complete the job [H].

TOMMY'S TIP

Don't leave the mortar mixing too long, or you'll be trying to lay bricks with candyfloss. If the barbecue is being built in fine sunny weather, give the bricks a good soaking before you start building, or the brick will soak up the moisture in the mortar before you've finished laying it. If the weather is poor, don't build it. Unfortunately, on television I have no choice – but you do!

ERECTING A SHED

Sheds – have you ever wondered just how many there are in this country? It's like cars! Just how many are there in circulation at the moment? At the risk of sounding controversially chauvinistic, historically sheds, like cars, have always been a bit of a bloke's thing. Fortunately, that's beginning to change, I add hastily! Just like cars, which are now designed to appeal to women as well, the same is happening to one of the last bastions of blokeness – the garden shed. It is no longer just the dismal chocolate-coloured, square, windowless box in the farthest corner of the garden, guaranteed to put off any woman from entering. In the past, the garden shed was a place where men could become boys again – where they could fantasize in solitude or with their mates. I even did a television show where a guy had turned the shed at the bottom of his garden into a proper little pub for himself and his bull terrier. He even named it 'The Dog's B*****ks'.

Sheds are now available with patio doors and verandahs. They can come with two storeys with windows and, dare I say it, pretty curtains. Nowadays they even make sheds for kids! Can you believe that? The garden shed used to be a man's bolthole, a place to escape the wife and kids! My uncle John says that if it keeps on like this, he's going to have to move back into the house to get any peace!

I built a shed. Even though I have only a tiny courtyard garden, I still had to have a shed. I built mine from scratch, not in kit form, and it was great until my wife became creative in the search for more room. I had to build in an extra freezer first, and as that was successful, I then had to make room for a second appliance – a tumble dryer, which left very little space for me.

I can understand people becoming animated over their own sheds, but I once had a guy getting excited over a shed I was erecting in somebody else's garden. I told him where to go and stick his own shed, the cheeky blighter, but unbeknown to me, Alan Titchmarsh popped round to his house to pacify him. If you are in any doubt regarding permission for a shed or outbuilding, contact your local authority for clarification.

TOMMY'S TIP

When you are constructing your shed, always ensure that the 100 x 100mm (4 x 4in) bearers are placed at 90° angles to the fixed joists on the underside of the floor. This will create a solid floor, with little deflection, so you won't bounce around all over the place every time you go in the shed!

A concrete screed is often the preferred base for a garden shed, but that can be a laborious and expensive way to create a base. If the shed has a wooden floor, as most of them do, ideally the shed should be slightly elevated off the ground to allow air to circulate underneath, as this prevents rot from setting in. For the television show, I devised a quick, cheap and simple method of creating a shed base support system.

Cut three concrete or breeze blocks (but not lightweight blocks), in half to form six pads. Position these at the four corners of the wooden floor section and two centrally beneath it. Using a spade, dig the pads in so the blocks remain just above the surface. Adjust the pads by packing or excavating to ensure

Tools Required:

Spade
Spirit level
Hammer
Cordless
drill/screwdriver
Tape measure

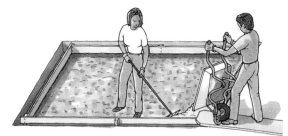

To lay a concrete base for a shed, dig out and thoroughly level the area it will cover. Erect wooden shuttering as a guide for the concrete. Mix the concrete, spread it and rake it level.

Once all the concrete has been poured into the space and raked level, use another board to tamp the surface absolutely flat by running the board across the top edges of the shuttering.

that they are all level, using a spirit level and board. Simply place the 100 x 100mm (4 x 4in) pressure-treated posts across the pads as bearers for the floor section [A].

Lay the floor section across the bearers [B] (no fixings required), and double-check for level.

The walls are next. If you don't have anyone to help you, support the first panel in place with an angled prop, while you screw fix through the bottom rail into the base. Position the second section and screw fix through the side rail [C], then do the same through the base rail and remove the prop. Simply attach the remaining panels in the same way. The roof is normally made into easy-fit sections, which slot into a rebate [D]. Screw fix through the rails to secure.

The felt is normally fixed in three sections, with the central ridge piece being fixed last over the two side sections and nailed down with galvanised clout nails to secure the felt [E]. This method ensures a waterproof lap, so take care not to damage the felt during construction.

Fascia boards are fitted to the front and rear elevations to keep the felt in place. The felt can be simply nailed with clout nails on either side, or turned under and fixed with a timber batten along its length (on the underside). You can attach a finial at either end to cover the fascia joints [F], with corner trims nailed to the four vertical corners to finish the job.

REPLACING THE FELT ON A SHED ROOF

Bear with me on this one! You may or may not know this, but I do love my football. Now, I don't mean just watching it, but also playing. Recently I was playing for Arsenal in a charity match. David Seaman said, 'I hear you play a bit, and are quite useful!' I said 'Pardon?' Although I heard him perfectly the first time, I just wanted to hear him say it again! On form as I was, I responded with 'Why, are you worried about your job?!' Oh, I forgot to tell you that I'm a goalkeeper as well, and I might well have been playing for England, except that I could never grow a ponytail long enough!

Talking of legends, I have played with some over the years. In fact, my most successful period of football was with two of the game's true greats – Terry Groombe and Tony Gallagher. Although basically good at it, they were both overweight due to post-match liquid consumption! However, under their captaincy and vice-captaincy, our team achieved what no other team in The Old Parmiterians' 102-year footballing history has ever achieved – a 100 percent season. We went through the whole season without losing or drawing a game, and won the treble.

Be patient, I'm slowly getting to the point. It's while I was involved in this charity football scene that I met and became friends with this very funny guy, who is passionate about football. His name is Mike Osman, he is a DJ on Capital Gold and he is one of the funniest men on radio. He has to be, as he supports Southampton! We often talk on the radio. It was during one of these conversations when a bet was struck on the results of the Southampton versus West Ham fixtures. Needless to say, I, as a supporter of the esteemed football academy West Ham, won both rounds last season. The stakes were raised for this season's first round: if I were to lose, I would have to do his garden. If Mike lost, he would have to do my roof – Mike being an ex-roofer. I thought it was a good bet and of course West Ham won. However, my jubilation disappeared when the materials arrived – two rolls of roofing felt and some clout nails. The so-and-so was just going to re-cover my shed roof and, as I hadn't specified which roof, he argued that it became his choice! On the next round of bets I'm going to completely tie him up, but knowing my luck, the Hammers will probably lose!

Begin by de-nailing the timber [A] and stripping off the old roof covering [B]. Make sure that you wear safety goggles and gloves when you are doing this. At the same time, you could take the opportunity to apply a coat of preservative to the timber roof panels.

Unroll the felt, measure the length required, and then mark and cut it with a craft knife and straightedge [C]. Always allow at least a couple of inches overhang at either end. Roll the cut lengths up again and roll out onto each side of the roof in turn [D], allowing an inch or two of overhang. Nail the felt along the ridge edge with galvanised clout nails to secure it [E]. Repeat on the other side.

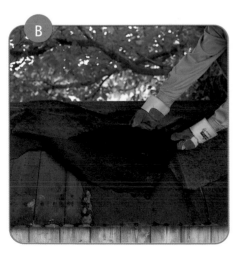

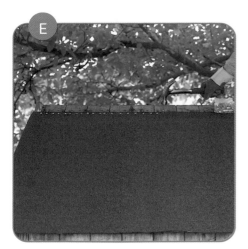

Tools Required:

Nail bar
Claw hammer
Pinchers
Scraper
Craft knife
Mastic gun
Straight edge
Safety glasses
Protective gloves

Cut the third section to size, allowing a minimum overlap of 50mm (2in) either side. This is called the ridge-capping piece. The ridge piece can be attached with clout nails or a mastic sealer adhesive. Apply the mastic beads with a mastic gun [F]. Roll out the felt and press it into place, working from the middle out [G]. Finally, nail all around the overhung edges to secure the felt covering from blowing off in the wind [H].

TOMMY'S TIP

If you have a leaky roof and you just don't have time to fix it properly, you could always suspend a tarpaulin or sheet of plastic above the shed roof as a temporary measure. It will act exactly like a giant umbrella, keeping everything dry until you have a chance to make the necessary repairs.

GLOSSARY

Airlock
A blockage in a pipe caused by a trapped bubble of air.

Appliance
A machine or device powered by electricity.

Architrave
The moulding around a window or door.

Back siphoning
The siphoning of part of a plumbing system caused by the failure of mains water pressure.

Baluster
One of a set of posts supporting a stair handrail.

Balustrade
The protective barrier along-side a staircase or landing.

Basecoat
A flat coat of paint over which a decorative glaze is applied.

Batt
A short cut length of glass-fibre or mineral-fibre insulant.

Batten
A narrow strip of wood.

Bore
The hollow part of a pipe.

Cap-nut
The nut used to tighten a fitting onto pipework.

Casing
The timber lining of a door or window opening.

Cavity wall
A wall made of two separate, parallel masonry skins with an air space between them.

Chamfer
A narrow flat surface along the edge of a workpiece – normally at an angle of 45 degrees to adjacent surfaces.

Chase
A groove cut in masonry or plaster to accept pipework or an electrical cable. Or: to cut or channel such grooves.

Circuit
A complete path through which an electric current can flow.

Concave
Curving inwards.

Conductor
A component, usually a length of wire, along which an electric current will pass.

Convex
Curving outwards.

Cornice
Continuous horizontal moulding between the walls and ceiling of a room.

Counterbore
To cut a hole that allows the head of a bolt or screw to lie below a surface.

Countersink
To cut a tapered recess that allows the head of a screw to be flush with a surface. Or: the tapered recess itself.

Coving
A prefabricated moulding used to make a cornice.

Cup
To bend as a result of shrinkage, specifically across the width of a piece of wood.

Dado
The lower part of an interior wall – usually defined by a moulded wooden rail at about waist height (the dado rail).

Damp-proof course
A layer of impervious material that prevents moisture rising through a concrete floor.

Drop
A strip of wallpaper measured and cut to length ready for pasting to a wall.

Earth
A connection between an electrical circuit and the earth (ground). Or: a terminal to which the connection is made.

Eaves
The edges of a roof that project beyond the walls.

Extension
A room or rooms added to an existing building.

Extension lead
A length of electrical flex for temporarily connecting the short permanent flex of an appliance to a wall socket.

Face edge
In woodworking, the surface which is planed square to the face side of the piece of work.

Face side
In woodworking, the flat planed surface from which other dimensions and angles are measured and worked.

Fascia
A strip of wood that covers the ends of rafters and to which external guttering is fixed.

Feather
To wear away or smooth an edge until it is undetectable.

Fence
An adjustable guide to keep the cutting edge of a tool a set distance from the edge of a workpiece.

Fuse board
Where the main electrical service cable is connected to the house circuitry. Or: the accumulation of consumer unit, meter, etc.

Galvanized
Covered with a protective coating of zinc.

Grain
The general direction of wood fibres. Or: the pattern produced on the surface of timber by cutting through the fibres.

Groove
A long narrow channel cut in plaster or wood in the general direction of the grain.

Grounds

Strips of wood fixed to a wall to provide nail-fixing points for skirting boards, door casings, etc.

Head plate

The top horizontal member of a stud partition.

Housing

A long narrow channel cut across the general direction of wood grain to form part of a joint.

Insulation

Materials used to reduce the transmission of heat or sound. Or: nonconductive material surrounding electrical wires or connections to prevent the passage of electricity.

Jamb

The vertical side of a doorframe or window frame.

Joist

A horizontal wooden or metal beam (such as an RSJ) used to support a structure such as a floor, ceiling or wall.

Key

To abrade a surface in order to provide a better grip when gluing something to it.

Knotting

Sealer, made from shellac, that prevents wood resin bleeding through a surface finish.

Knurled

Impressed with a series of fine grooves designed to improve the grip, for instance a knurled knob or handle on a tool.

Lintel

A horizontal beam used to support the wall over a door or window opening.

Mastic

A nonsetting compound used to seal joints.

Mitre

A joint formed between two pieces of wood by cutting bevels of equal angle at the ends of each piece. Or: to cut the joint.

Pallet

A wooden plug built into masonry to provide a fixing point for a door casing.

Pilot hole

A small-diameter hole drilled prior to the insertion of a woodscrew to act as a guide for its thread.

Primer

The first coat of a paint system applied to protect wood or metal.

Profile

The outline or contour of an object.

PTFE

Polytetrafluoroethylene – a material used to make tape for sealing threaded plumbing fittings.

Purlin

A horizontal beam that provides intermediate support for rafters or sheet roofing.

Rafter

One of a set of parallel sloping beams that form the main structural element of a roof.

Rebate

A stepped rectangular recess along the edge of a workpiece, usually forming part of a joint. Or: to cut such recesses.

Residual current device

A device that monitors the flow of electrical current through the live and neutral wires of a circuit.

Reveal

The vertical side of an opening.

Riser

The vertical part of a step.

Rising main

The pipe that supplies water under mains pressure, usually to a storage tank in the roof.

Rolled steel joist (RSJ)

A steel beam, usually with a cross section in the form of a capital letter I.

Sash

The openable part of a window.

Score

To scratch a line with a pointed tool.

Scribe

To copy the profile of a surface on the edge of sheet material that is to be butted against it. Or: to mark a line with a pointed tool.

Sheathing

The outer layer of insulation on an electrical cable or flex.

Short circuit

The accidental re-routing of electricity to earth, which increases the flow of current and blows a fuse.

Stud partition

A timber frame interior dividing wall.

Studs

The vertical members of a timber frame wall.

Tamp

To pack down firmly with repeated blows.

Template

A cut-out pattern made from paper, wood, metal, etc., to help shape a workpiece accurately.

Terminal

A connection to which the bared ends of electrical cable or flex are attached.

Thinner

A solvent, such as turpentine, used to dilute paint or varnish.

Trap

A bent section of pipe below a bath, sink, etc. It contains standing water to prevent the passage of gases.

Tread

The horizontal part of a step.

Undercoat

A layer or layers of paint used to obliterate the colour of a primer and build up a protective body of paint before the top coat is applied. (See the Paint Chart on pages 14–15.)

INDEX

ACKNOWLEDGEMENTS

Firstly to my wife Marie, for those constant cups of tea,
and for putting up with me when I'm tired!
Tinks and John for their able assistance.
Richard and Jimmy (joinery).
George, Tony and Terry (plumbing and electrical).
Gloria and Dave at 'Café Booze' (aptly named), for
hearty breakfasts and liquid sustenance during
in-depth research!
Maggie for her wonderful bagels.
Willie and Kalem for steering the ship without me!
Angela, Myles, Luke and all at HarperCollins.
And of course my producer Carol Haslam, for putting
me on this rollercoaster in the first place.
The guiding hands of my agents Annie,
Debbie and Luigi.

Step Editions would like to thank the following companies for providing tools and equipment for this book:

Tools & fixings
Screwfix Direct
Tel. 0500 414141
www.screwfix.com

Hire tools
Hewden Plant Hire
Tel. 0161 8488621

Fireplace
Winther Browne
Fine Wood Carvings and Mouldings
Nobel Road
Eley Estate
Edmonton
London
N18 3DX
Tel. 020 8884 6000

Paint
Dulux Decorator Centres
Tel. 0161 9683000

Tiles
Johnson Tiles
PO Box 1742
Stoke on Trent
ST6 4SF
Tel. 01782 575575
www.johnson-tiles.com

Patio slabs
Bradstone
Hulland Ward
Ashbourne
Derbyshire
DE6 3ET
Tel. 0800 975 9828
www.bradstone.com

Bricks
Hanson Brick
Stewartby
Bedford
MK43 9LZ
Tel. 08705 258258
www.hanson-brickseurope.com

Also many thanks to the following individuals for their help in the production of this book: Tim Ridley; Jakki Dearden; Mark Petts at Screwfix; Steve and Claire Green; Michael and Sue Read; June Parham; Sue Wilson.